Investments with Dividends

Cliff Booth

Crest Publishers
P.O. Box 595   •
Chelsea, Alabama 35043

i

Copyright © Pending 2016 by Cliff Booth
P.O. Box 595
Chelsea, Alabama 35043
(205) 527-7785
crestpublishers@gmail.com

ISBN: 978-1-939960-22-1

Printed in the United States of America

For

Kate and AJ

Anna Elizabeth and Alice

My Investors

George and Doris Bagwell

Jerry Bobo

Coach Lohrone Cannon

Bobbie Cherones

Dr. Bruce Chesser

Judge Paul Conger

Don Crowe

Buster and Margie Hallman

Ronald Lett

Coach Ray Nelson

Rev. Tony Preston

J.C. Randolph

Dr. Joyce Sellers

Lyn Slattery

Mickey and Wilma Smith

Talmedge "Smitty" Smith

Paul Thompson

Bobby Walker

Rev. Bill Yarber

Fayette First Baptist Church – Fayette, AL

Calvary Baptist Church – Tuscaloosa, AL

Foreword

The meaning of life is to find your gift. The purpose of life is to give it away.

William Shakespeare

Life is an adventure, a journey, an expedition. My life certainly confirms Shakespeare's statement that most all of us search for our gift. The journey involves multiple avenues and crossroads where decisions based on faith, determination, encouragement, and guidance provide us with opportunities to search for and to find our special gift. The road I have travelled has had many twists and turns, but each experience led me to my goal to find my gift and my purpose in life.

On the journey, I found the encouragement and willingness from others to invest in and to guide me toward my goal. In my own mind, which is all that matters, I have discovered both my gift and my purpose. My gift is the art of teaching and learning. My journey in education started at Bevill State Community College and at the University of Alabama in 1987. The success I experienced teaching high school from 1989 until 1996 fueled my confidence to become a leader in education. The people who encouraged and supported my journey into administration possessed many of the same characteristics as the men and women who invested in me as a child growing up in poverty and those that supported me in changing my career.

For one school year in 1997, I returned to my hometown and was the assistant principal at Fayette Elementary School. I found myself in the company of those with whom I had grown up. Many were the children of those who had invested in me as a child and teenager. Once again, the support from those who knew me best was encouraging, so I began my education administration on a positive note. I experienced the same growth in experience and knowledge as the assistant principal at Riverside Junior High School for three years, which prepared me for the position of Principal at Holt High School for eight years.

I have since served as a transportation director in Tuscaloosa County, another term as a high school principal, and a director for Morgan County schools in North Alabama. In all my experiences, my passion has remained strong to my calling as both a practitioner and an advocate for effective teaching and learning. Compelled by my experiences, associations, and observations, I feel the time has come to put my gratitude to so many and my experiences from so much into a book that focuses on finding our gifts and seeing the gifts of others.

My writing in no way proposes any new ideas about teaching and learning. However, it does reflect on fundamentals abandoned in recent years but needs reintroducing to a new generation of teachers and leaders in education. My purpose in life is to share my experiences and ideas to help others see how and why we teach are as important as what we teach.

Chauncey,
Thank you for
all you do. Best
Wishes and great
dividends from good
investments.

INVESTMENTS WITH DIVIDENDS

One

My journey in life and career has been diverse, and the experiences from both are intertwined and inseparable, with each domain complementing the other. During my childhood and teenage years, I was encouraged from the investment of many people and groups that took interest in and motivated me to reach my potential. In addition, the experience I gained from a variety of situations and employment taught me valuable lessons about learning and attaining success. My career path has involved returning to college and eventually earning three degrees and teaching in a high school classroom. I have also served as an assistant principal in an elementary and junior high school, leading a high school as principal for twelve years, being appointed to an interim term as a transportation director, and currently serving as a Human Resources, Alternative Programs, and Secondary Instruction Director. Each position has afforded me the opportunity to grow, mature, and develop a better understanding of many aspects of public education. I have enjoyed and grown professionally in every position, and I am extremely satisfied with the several roles for which I am currently responsible. I have discovered that where I am in my career is a culmination of personal experiences, along with the investments by so many people in my life. The experiences and investments have resulted in substantial dividends for me and hopefully my profession.

My journey to a career in education is the result of multiple factors in my life that had profound effects on me but none more profound than the investments in me made by so many individuals. It was my personal experiences and the investments from others that drew me to return to school and change careers at age thirty-two. My experiences and investments continue to affect me in my newest position in charge of personnel and secondary instruction. No matter our position in education, our ultimate responsibility is investing in children by focusing on teaching and learning. No matter the position I have held, my interest, dedication, and passion have always focused on effective ways to help teachers provide the most effective instruction that results in improving student achievement. I have reached a point in my life and career to reflect on the many events and people I have encountered on the unique path I have travelled. It probably sounds conceited, but I consider myself a wise person because of my various positive and negative experiences. Our culture and society have changed, and I feel I have changed in response to experiences and changes in my personal life. Just as all of us change in response to our experiences and the culture around us, education must change to invest in children by adapting to changes in students, parents, job markets, as well as social issues in order for the United States to continue to lead the world in creativity and innovation.

Get in the Car

The technology improvements made in the last twenty-five years are surpassed only by the improvements that will occur in the next twenty years, as change is not only inevitable, but the pace of change is increasing exponentially. The change in technology is an example of a multitude of recent and future changes in our society and in education. All of us strive to provide for our children all that we can in order for them to enjoy life and prosper more than we have. I am very proud of two daughters. Their mother and I worked hard to expose them to learning opportunities and experiences to help them discover their interests and talents. As a result, each has become successful. My oldest daughter was always studious and focused on achieving superior grades and performing academically ahead of her peers. Today, she is a successful pharmacist and mother of two beautiful daughters of her own. My youngest was less inclined to soar academically, but was always a leader and willing to think and act outside the box. She is a very successful middle school English teacher who uses innovative, creative, and engaging teaching practices that motivate her students to love learning. Since we are almost identical in our philosophies about teaching and learning, we often confide in each other, and I seek her advice as much as she calls and ask me for my opinion. She has a daughter who has just started kindergarten and one-year-old son who is a big change for a predominantly female family.

As a re-entering college student, I was able to practice and demonstrate on my daughters every methodology about learning I discovered at the University of Alabama. I inundated Jenny and Julie with experiments I read and learned about in educational psychology classes. Both learned to think and problem solve, probably from the exposure to educated and vocal parents. Although my parents expressed interest in and stressed the importance of a good education, my brother and I learned more about developing a strong work ethic and being productive in whatever we decided to do. In essence, I learned best the value of hard work, and my children learned to use their talents and learning to develop skills and abilities necessary to work with their heads and not their backs. Additionally, we did instill in our children the value of hard work, which helped them to achieve even more success. I recall that Jenny often worked twelve-hour shifts at CVS while pregnant with both children.

My daughters are now raising their own offspring, and Papa watches closely to see the differences and similarities between the two about rearing children. It is interesting to compare the similarities and differences in the behaviors and expectations I had for my children to those who are teaching my grandchildren. One thing is perfectly clear- my children are different from their parents, and their children are different from them. What are the differences and what impact will my children's investment in my grandchildren have on their direction in life, and what investments will schools make to prepare them?

During my pre-teen and early teen years, my community friends and I were active and always interested in finding something to keep us occupied and entertained. Most of our activities involved hunting, fishing, swimming, and playing a variety of sports based on the sport season.

Except for brief periods of summer baseball, there were no organized activities. Therefore, my friends and I had to develop our own devices and creativity to collaborate among ourselves and develop our plans. As one can imagine, those discussions were often heated and sometimes resulted in arguments leading to actual fighting. Most of the time, however, we came to a mutual agreement but usually with dissenting views. The point is that we had to discuss and plan our activities without supervision from parents or community coaches. As a result, we had to think, communicate without electronic devices, organize, and implement a variety of options that would occupy us for several hours or until time to go home, eat, and go to bed. During the summer months when school was not in session, when we grew tired of baseball in the pasture or yard, swimming, fishing, or whatever, we had to reconvene as a group and reorganize and plan our next adventure. We were constantly developing and using multiple skills that sharpened our problem-solving and thinking skills - plus how to work as a group, work through disagreements, and come to a common consensus about what activity in which we would participate. Now, contrast these activities to what kids in this age group are now involved.

It is difficult for anyone to dispute the effect that organized activities have had on the current school-aged child. Organized community and school athletic leagues provide children with organized athletic events for almost every day of the year. In recent years, there has been a proliferation of female sport involvement. In some cases, parents and kids have made the decision to concentrate on one sport. Specifically soccer, baseball, basketball, lacrosse, and golf have become year round sports for many students. In addition, dance, karate, music, and theatre absorb after school time for parents and their children. The role of the parent, even working parents, has become extremely demanding as far as time, money, and commitment. Talk to any modern parent with children of school age and eventually the top subject will inevitably move to activities of their children. Whether the family is involved in multiple activities or a singular concentration, daily travel and participation require a tremendous amount of time spent traveling and participating in activities.

I love sports, and I think children and parents exploring extracurricular activities realize how important they are to physical and social development. However, in many cases the expectations of parents and the development of their child into the next superstar are more often than not unrealistic and often require excess amounts of time and energy. Not including monetary cost, the time spent compared to the amount of return is not a very attractive investment. Interestingly, Archie Manning never allowed Peyton or Eli to participate in organized sports until middle school. I think they turned out just fine.

Perhaps the least observed result of so many more activities for children is that children no longer have to plan and organize games and activities - their parents, coaches, churches and others are doing all the planning for them. Actually, all of us are investing in our children's futures, but we may be inhibiting them at the same time. I often observe and listen as parents discuss plans for the afternoons and weekends. The activities require a great deal of organization and planning in order to get from one event to another. Parents develop schedules for their children to be at this and that place for events that often start immediately after school and can go late into the evening. As a principal, most of the complaints from parents I have had regarding homework or other assignments were often argued as an interference with parents and their plans - too little time and too much to do. The child in all these activities jumps in the car, stops for a quick dinner, and is carried to the activity - all planned, organized, and orchestrated by the parent. Children no longer have to think. Their parents, coaches, youth group leader, and yes teachers bombard the child with dates, times, and activities that require nothing from the child except to get in and out of the car. Most of our parents warned us of all the things we should not do. Today, parents instruct the kids on all they are to do.

My point is that in spite of all our good intentions at providing all the things to our children that we wish we had had, we have taken away their ability to think, plan, and solve problems on their own. Parents, coaches, and teachers now have to do all the thinking. Children just get in the car and ride. We will never be great as long as we fail to invest in opportunities for students to think and problem-solve.

Just Give Me the Answer - Please

Children, and for that matter all students, including my graduate students I teach in leadership classes, look for the simplest and most expedient way to check off requirements, assignments, and other obstacles standing between them and the academic credit they desire to move to the next obstacle. As a graduate and undergraduate student, I often started work on the class syllabus the day I received it from my instructor. I even created a checklist of courses for each degree I have earned in order to visualize the progress I was making toward graduation and another degree. It is our nature to follow steps and get to where we want to go in the most energy- efficient way possible. Not many people intentionally take scenic routes on the way to our destination. We are obsessed with getting to our destination quickly and easily. My wife often pokes fun at me for getting to wherever I am going a minimum of fifteen minutes early. It seems at times there is an internal clock in me that is constantly going off with plenty of time to spare. Interestingly, my brother who was a year younger than me was always late, and I mean ALWAYS and LATE, to everything. He passed away much too early a few years back. That was probably the only thing he ever did early. He also made it to his own funeral on time - because I was in charge of all the arrangements. God bless you brother, I really miss you. In any event, it is in most of our DNA to rush and get things accomplished, and is what I refer to as an assembly-line mentality.

I was fortunate after high school that a great man I grew to respect called me. Smitty was the market manager in the meat department in the local A&P grocery store. I have no clue how he got my name and made the decision to call me, but I surely am glad he did. For the next five years, I worked in the market and learned a trade that I still enjoy whenever a chicken or ham needs carving on holidays. I worked in the A&P part-time and started classes at the local community college. After a year in the market learning how to quickly cut up and prepare chickens, pork, and beef, a learning experience that perfectly suited my assembly-line mentality, I got the great idea of going to work full-time at the big unionized automobile muffler plant. My reasoning was to work an eight-hour shift from 3:00 in the afternoon until midnight and go to school during the day. In case you may have not heard, teenagers and young adults require a tremendous amount of sleep. I soon found myself sleeping in and missing my morning classes. The realization that I had bitten off more than I was able to chew was causing serious doubts to selfish decision to work longer and make more money. I was also finding out about real assembly-line work.

Arvin Industries produced new and replacement mufflers and tailpipes for automobiles. It was an economic leader and major employer in my small hometown. Many men and a few women had successful careers and were able to enjoy a very good income right out of high school. Most of the work at the plant was at a station on a line bending, welding, and preparing products for shipment to distributors around the United States. My job was on a tailpipe line, picking up a tailpipe coming down a conveyor line, placing the pipe in a press set to bend the pipe into a proper shape, and replacing the pipe on the conveyor and then picking up the next one coming down the line. Repeatedly the process continued and time stood still! Very often, the conveyor would stop due to a malfunction and all workers were required to stand at their station until repairs to the problem were complete - sometimes the entire shift was spent standing at the conveyor and doing nothing. Breaks and dinner were at precise times and explicit intervals. Failure to be in position at appropriate times meant a reprimand and dismissal if the infraction continued - unless you were a union worker, which took three years to acquire. Two weeks was all I could take. It was the most mindless and unskilled labor I had ever performed. Having no ambition, problem-solving skills, and desire to accomplish anything except to make a good living were the only job requirements. I went back to the A&P to talk to Smitty.

I told Smitty that I had made a very bad mistake and asked if there was any way he could arrange to hire me back. With a grin that reflected his years of experience in business as well as life, he informed me that he never turned in my letter of resignation and that I had simply been on vacation. Smitty could have found many young guys for the position, but he invested in me and was wise enough to know that young people often make mistakes. For whatever reason, he did not give up on his investment and kept the door opportunity open for me.

I immediately went to the plant to inform my supervisor of my intention to leave the company. In an effort to be understanding I suppose, he congratulated me on being a very fine machine operator and that I could have been a very good employee for the future. Although I pretended to be flattered by his praise of my machine operator abilities, I had concluded that a trained chimp could do the job I had been assigned. If the plant were still operating today, a robot would be doing the job. The mindless yet high-paying assembly line jobs are gone. As educators, we must now prepare students for higher skilled jobs as the traditional middle class jobs are disappearing and as a result, the middle class population continues shrink. Yet our education systems have continued to stress recall brain functions and have ignored the need to teach kids to think and solve perplexing problems. Nothing illustrates our misguided focus in education more than the *No Child Left Behind Act* (NCLB) of 2001).

Gather Your Family and Head to the Hills - The Russians and the Feds Are Coming!

Until 1957, education in the United States consisted almost solely on the factory method, with students, based on their age, assigned to grade levels and maneuvered through the grades until the final product was a high school graduate with fundamental skills such as reading, writing, and arithmetic - popularly known as the 3Rs. The quality of the product produced measured the achievement on a grading scale from failure to excellent. Students sat in rows and listened to teachers talk, and they sometimes demonstrated the memorization of facts and dates. There are those today who advocate that we return to the 3Rs. While we are at it, let's plow up all the highways, tear down all the bridges, ground all the airplanes, dispose of all the medical advances, and remove all the other improvements that have occurred in the last 100 years.

Our scope of learning broadened on October 4, 1957, when the Soviet Union launched Sputnik 1. As in most cases, fear of demise led presidents, Congress, and educators to act quickly to eliminate the perceived technological gap between the two superpowers of the world. The new emphasis, based on fear and anxiety, was to become better in areas most

14

associated with technological advancement as we fought to catch up with our nemesis, the communist Soviet Union. In a bold and adventurous proclamation in 1960, newly elected president John Kennedy proclaimed the United States would put a man on the moon before the end of the decade, and the race was on. Schools now expanded teaching and learning in science and math in an attempt to alleviate the threat to national security. It was a positive step and a result of the changes in the social, technological, and political culture of the times. With the creation of agencies such as NASA and the National Science Foundation (NSF), federal involvement in education took the first step toward a national emphasis on education.

During the sixties, all of us experienced the fear from the threat of the Soviet Union. I vividly remember films in school on nuclear bombs and the resulting fallout of radiation. We participated in drills, huddling under our desks - a futile attempt to survive a nuclear explosion. I recall lying in bed at night considering the effects of an attack and trying to formulate in my young mind a way to avoid the inevitable. It is hard to imagine as I observe the children and youth of today that I was so aware of the possibility of such a disaster at a young age. The Cuban Missile Crisis only compounded that fear, along with the assassination of a president, and the daily television reports of American casualties from the Vietnam War. Even the current terrorist threats and events of September 11, 2001, do not reach the magnitude of concern and fear of those of us from that generation. Sure, massive school shootings in Columbine, Newtown, and too many other places concern all of us, but there was something different about the turmoil of the sixties that is different from the events of today. Perhaps we are distracted from worldly events by all the opportunities we have to involve ourselves in personal endeavors. Maybe we have become desensitized as events have become commonplace and by the amount of information flowing from the internet or twenty-four hour news programs. It may be a good thing that our children do not worry about threats and challenges as we did – or maybe not.

We hold these truths to be self-evident...

Being a child and a public school student during the sixties, I was keenly aware of changes that I witnessed in our social and political culture. Listening to our parents, reading the paper, and listening to Walter Cronkite helped me develop a sharp interest in history that was happening all

16

around me. On a more personal level, I began to see the changes also.

My maternal grandfather had a profound effect on me as a young boy. Papa sold coal to the public and had several black employees who loaded and delivered coal to houses. The relationship that we had with the workers was odd by today's standards. The home-based business resembled a busy town with multiple activities each day. My grandmother prohibited the black workers from ever entering the house. She made lunch every day, and on rare occasions, the workers ate a plate of home cooking prepared for them and delivered to the back porch. I also recall signs at the Dairy King at the takeout windows labeled for blacks and whites. At the courthouse, where we often went on Saturdays to go to the bathroom while shopping at the Dime Store or waiting for a movie at the theatre, there were water fountains and restrooms for whites and blacks. Papa could not read or write, and I remember as a young reader my astonishment when he often drank from the black fountain or entered the black restroom. Even at a very young age, I saw all of this troubling and a bit odd. I could not express why it felt strange, it just did. The beginning of the Civil Rights movement put me in a position between the established cultural establishment reinforced by all my family and the uneasiness I had with the accepted social norms. Often, children face the most direct social change because they are generally more inclined to accept change. Is it any wonder that schools are often the battlegrounds for movements that challenge the status quo?

For decades preceding the Civil Rights movement, education like most of American society functioned under the philosophy of *separate but equal* regarding racial diversity and segregation. My grandmother providing lunch for a black worker on the back porch was a simple example of the dubious philosophy to justify segregation of the races. Although the landmark Supreme Court case of *Brown vs. Board of Education* outlawed racial discrimination in American schools, it would be years until the effects of the ruling would come to fruition in schools. In the South, and especially in Alabama, leave it to football to be a catalyst for change in racial discrimination. It has been argued that the University of Alabama's legendary football coach Paul "Bear" Bryant's decision to add The University of Southern California to its 1970 football schedule had as much effect on desegregating college and high schools as Dr. King's appeal for equality. Getting trounced by the USC team with two black players in 1970, along with a 41-14 thumping by rival Tennessee with two black players in 1969, illustrated to fans in the South and in the nation that black athletes were going to transform athletics and break down walls of discrimination that were embedded in the social structure.

My high school first allowed black students to enroll in 1970, and with the move came our first black football player. Stephen, affectionately known as "Lightning" because of his speed and agility, opened the gates of integration and soon the school and the team became fully integrated with black students and athletes providing the stimulus for social change in the school and the community. I saw the transformation first hand as the students brought an entirely new dimension to the halls of the school and on the practice field. Even football road trips saw the effects of an emotional, enthusiastic, fun-loving, and affectionate inversion of an often-misunderstood social structure that existed in the black community. When we won a game, the trip home on the bus was like nothing any of us had ever witnessed. New cheers, chants, and other exhibitions of joy and satisfaction with a good performance created a sense of comradely among all the payers - black and white. Athletes were the trailblazers to a new social structure developing in the country - another indication of the importance of schools as a vehicle for change. No longer would the white students drive over to the black school on game nights to watch the game and the band perform. The African-American students were now with us and the struggle would continue as the evolution to a more racially equal society continues to present the nation with problems and opportunities to improve the lives for all of us. Education would also have to change in response to the outside challenge of the Soviet Union, but just as importantly to the challenge of more diversified populations of students in public schools. Increasingly, the federal government's role in assuring accommodations and equality to all students would require investing in the landscape of American schools, resulting in increased funding from Washington, contingent upon guidelines and mandates from Congress and the Supreme Court.

Two

A major inhibitor to the goals of policymakers and educators to improve our country by providing opportunities for young people to learn and prepare for productive citizenship is the tendency for children to follow in the paths of their parents. We often use terms like "breaking the cycle of poverty" when dealing with students from low income families. There is also a "cycle of prosperity" illustrated by the fact that children with affluent and successful parents generally turn out to be successful. Although there are exceptions, high-income communities have schools that are the highest achieving, and low-income neighborhoods have the poorest performing schools. Many argue that the tax money provided to local schools from their communities determines the achievement success, or lack thereof, of the schools. Research shows that resources and money alone do not make a school successful. Many attempts from government sources, and in some cases private funding, have failed to produce significant results in a school's performance. A popular and more valid argument today is that the more prosperous schools employ the best teachers and administrators. Although I think there is some truth in the assumption, I consider the notion more correlation than causation. My conclusion is that there are many factors that can have an effect on student achievement and school success, but the factor with the most influence is also the most elusive - a passion for learning derived from investments, expectations, ambition, and motivation - developed from parents and families and nurtured in schools.

Somewhat ironically, the most difficult challenges we face in life are the times that build character and make us better. I grew up in a small town in a one-parent house, and to say my mother struggled to makes ends meet would be a drastic understatement. The house where we grew up was a literal log house that was 150 years old when we lived there. With incredibly uneven floors, low ceilings, no interior doors, and a fireplace with a rock and mud chimney, it would best be described fondly in modern terms as primitive. To this day, when people refer to housing, art, or other areas as primitive in a charming or enticing way, I recall my childhood and have no desire to be in any way drawn to the fad. My brother and I wore clothes from the dollar store and despite their poor value, were clean - a result of Saturday trips to town and hours spent at the laundromat, as mother washed and dried our clothes. I was sixteen years old before we were able to get a washer and dryer. Mother's car was always old and used, and we were constantly dealing with the usual used car expenses to keep it running. Mother purchased food at the local community store owned by her distant cousin. She charged our food bill each afternoon and paid on Friday when she got her check. I recall many times when an unexpected financial challenge forced her to carry-over part or all of the week's expenses to the next, despite the grumbling and dissatisfaction from the storeowner. However, somewhere down deep, there was a kind heart in the man, and we were able to avoid going hungry.

When I was ten years old, mother made a decision that I believe most assuredly changed my direction in life. As a young child, I had gone to our small country church where my grandfather sat on the second row and was often heard to affirm the preacher's comments with an "amen." I also remember as a four year old a few brief reflections of the funeral when mother had to deal with the loss of a seventeen-year-old child from a previous marriage that died in a car wreck. My half-sister, along with Papa, my grandmother, mother, and several other relatives are buried in the cemetery at the church. Therefore, it was a big step when mother decided for the best interest of Joe and me, we would start attending the First Baptist Church in town. Mother worked at the garment factory with several friends who attended First Baptist, and hearing about the youth and other activities the big church was able to offer, she concluded that to improve the chances for the salvation of her two young boys we should change churches. Suddenly, with our poor quality clothes, embarrassing housing, and rattletrap car, we stepped into a social environment of people who were much more financially fortunate than we were. Nevertheless, these people were good to us and were willing to invest in us. They welcomed us, and Joe and I were soon included in many activities at the church. I am not sure to this day the motive of the people who took in a family who struggled in many ways. I believe a big part of their acceptance was the result of a truly genuine Christian spirit of love and caring for all people. Maybe also, the people saw in us something that we did not see in ourselves. We were, in fact, reasonably intelligent and suffered from no criminal acts or other questionable associations. I can say without reservation that the people of First Baptist never seemed condescending, disrespectful, or unloving. They were kind and encouraging and provided the kind of direction we needed in order to break a cycle of poverty and realize the opportunity we had to become successful. The church would be a dramatic influence on me until my mid-thirties. I firmly believe that schools can have the same impact on students today. In essence, there was an intervention and an investment in my life that not only gave me an avenue for improvement in my life. It also instilled in me a great deal of motivation and awakened my ambition to succeed. Not only did those around me expect me to break the cycle and each was willing to invest in it, I now had that expectation of myself.

My church family continued to hold me accountable, and I met my first wife and the mother of my two beautiful daughters at the church. Both my children grew up and were baptized in the church, and I was ordained as a deacon. I had become a member of the church family that had played the most significant role in changing my course in life. The confidence I gained in myself, with the encouragement from my family and friends, would help me realize my calling in life and set the stage for a remarkable career in education. Although finding my direction would come later in life at the age of thirty-two, it came with a passion and confidence I had gained from my experiences in the workforce, but my faith and the encouragement, guidance, and motivation from others were the main sources of the awakening.

In 1974, I withdrew from the University of Alabama and went to work full-time with A&P. Although the ambition and determination awakened in me, I had not acquired the full revelation of my calling, and the vision of a very good paycheck enticed me to give up on a college education. It only took a couple of years to realize the income was not worth the stress associated with an occupation and a company that led to a dead end. My wife's family was successful and farmed several thousand acres of cotton and soybeans. I saw the opportunity to be part of a successful business as possibly a way to satisfy my ambition to be financially and personally successful. Therefore, I turned my resignation in at the A&P, moved my wife and myself into a mobile home, and went to work on the farm. For the next twelve years, I pretended to be a farmer and an executive manager. Up until my return to school later, the years were the most educational in my life. My then father-in-law was like a father to me. He taught me about hard work, being financially prudent, and dealing with adversity. Although we did not see eye to eye on almost everything, he had a profound effect on me, and I will always be grateful for his patience as well as his hardheaded direction. I am most appreciative of his investment in me. As I reflect, my most profound achievement as a farmer, other than the practical skills associated with self-employment, was to see the big picture, along with how to organize and plan in order to achieve the most efficient way to produce a product. During this time, my two daughters were born, and I became more mature in my spirituality and concerned about what I wanted to achieve in my life. The maturity led me to dig deep into my heart, seeking to find what role life destined me to play - it was not to be a farmer.

Teaching a youth Sunday school class and working with my wife who had decided to get a teaching degree, I discovered a talent and passion for teaching. I found that I had a way of communicating with young people, and I began to develop a philosophy about learning based on my experiences. I began to feel the calling, and I talked with anyone who would listen and help me in making one of the most significant decisions I would make in my life. At some point, I would have to talk to my father-in-law, with whom I was now a partner in the business. I was not looking forward to the discussion. He was the most practical and wise man I had ever known, but stoic and businesslike. I felt he would see no practicality in a decision for me to leave the business in pursuit of a dubious career dealing with children in a profession that he felt was corrupt and dysfunctional.

Mechanically Learning Disabled

During the summers in high school, I worked on the farm for my future father-in-law. I have discussed many of the events of my childhood and teenage years and how numerous events helped shape my life. Without any doubt, the most traumatic events that would initially discourage my development and almost defeat me were the three summers I worked on the farm. I had been around some machinery as a child at my grandfather's coal yard, and many times I sat in the middle of the seat in the coal truck and changed gears for him. However, the trucks, tractors, combines, and cotton pickers on the farm went well beyond any experience I had had before. Contrast my experience and abilities as one who was considered by all the workers as being a total idiot when it came to operating machinery, with those of my future brothers-in-law who had been driving tractors and cultivating crops since they were nine years old. Everything I did seemed to turn into disaster in the form of wrecked trucks, stuck tractors, and other damaged equipment. I would have probably fired myself if I had been in charge of someone doing as much damage as I did. However, since the Randolphs were a part of the church family that in effect had adopted me, along with the unfortunate fact in their minds that I was dating their daughter, I remained employed. My father-in-law assigned me to less destructive and dangerous jobs such as pulling a water wagon with a pickup truck for the crusty old man with no compassion or encouragement in his soul. His job was to spray chemicals to kill cockleburs and Johnson grass in the cotton fields. As fate would have it, even this job turned out to be an adventure for me. The old wagon had bad wheels that regularly ran off and left me stranded, often in the absolute middle of nowhere. I continued assignments to other jobs from time to time considered safe for me, but every time I had to get around machinery, one could count on disaster at any time. I am reminded of what Einstein said "... if you judge a fish by its ability to climb a tree it will live its whole life believing it's stupid." Moreover, I was beginning to feel very stupid.

My lack of ability in activities associated with farming proved a source of amusement and a popular topic of discussion for my eventual family by marriage and business partners. When I made mistakes, I often heard the comments under the breath and saw the amusement and oftentimes abandonment of hope for improvement in the eyes of the family and coworkers. The youngest brother was less reserved than the others were, and often spoke aloud what the others were thinking about me. I would often quiz my future wife about her family discussions at the dinner table regarding her boyfriend's adventures during the day at work. My confidence in myself wilted, and insecurity fostered even more daily failures in my performance on the farm. Although I wanted to perform well, my constant failure created a personal negative attitude about my abilities and myself. Although I would one day overcome that attitude, the insecurity and fear of failure would continue to haunt me - even to this day.

It is interesting to compare my performance in an environment that was lacking in familiarity and lack of natural talent to the experiences that many children have in the classroom. Some students are just naturally good at school. Naturally, good students are easy to teach, and most teachers enjoy working with them. However, less talented students present teachers with challenges that many are not able or willing to confront because it makes the job more difficult and time-consuming. In my opinion, by the time these students arrive in middle and high school, they have become perplexed, disillusioned, and often broken. Many begin to consider themselves as failures and resort to poor behavior, academic apathy, and withdrawal in order to avoid the embarrassment of not being able to perform with their peers. It is easy for me to associate my feelings of failure in my summer experiences in farming to the kids who do not perform well in school. As educators, we should be careful about judging students too quickly. Most often, we tend to equate school performance with academic ability. To me, this may be one of our greatest shortfalls in education. The fact is there are many parents and children who are very good at "playing school." They know all the ways to "jump through hoops" in order to get a good grade. It is amazing that so much of what we call learning is not actually learning but knowing how to play the game.

The workers I got to know during the summer on the farm and became even more familiar with later when I worked full-time, were very good men who worked hard, were very skilled at farm work, and performed as directed most of the time. All of them had very limited formal education, and some struggled to read a few words. Unfortunately, each of them had to be told precisely how and what to do, even though I determined most were very good at problem solving and thinking ahead. These men were afraid of making mistakes and were accustomed to plans being spelled out to them in outrageous detail - including exactly what to do, as well as how and when to do it. My father-in-law was a very intelligent man with a mechanical engineering mind and explained daily the individual process and outcome he expected from each worker. He often had the worker repeat the procedure to him when he was finished explaining. As with many students, the workers were very good at playing the game. Although the men were capable of much more when given the opportunity, there was hardly ever the opportunity, and eventually they lost the ability and will to think on their own.

Breaking Cycles

As educators, we often see in students what they do not see in themselves. My daughter explains the lack of reasoning of most teenagers is the result of the delayed development of the prefrontal cortex, which is the part of the brain that reasons. On most individuals, the development is not mature until the age of twenty-eight! Moreover, the part of the brain that encourages taking risks is fully mature in middle school students. Is it any wonder we see poor decision-making on the part of students in our schools? Although many of my teachers in high school mentioned that I could be a much better student, my reasoning was that

there were more important things to occupy my interest -
mainly sports, outdoor activities, and the opposite sex. As a
result, I was an average student in high school. How often
has a teacher and administrator observed the same
afflictions in students and tried to reason with them?
However, the message hardly ever gets through to them and
generally ignored.

When I made the decision to go back to school at the
age of thirty-two, I faced the uncertainty that I would suffer
from the same malady that held me back in high school and
my first attempt at college. Therefore, I decided to stick my
toe in the water first and enrolled for one political science
class at the local community college. I had explained my
uncertainty of success to my father-in-law to cover myself in
case I did fail. I also did not want him to think I was
abandoning him all at once. A great deal of thought and
reasoning went into the approach I had taken to return to a
college class and how to justify the decision to my business
partner and father-in-law. His response was the usual stoic
glance, and he was in no way encouraging or discouraging.
My response in the class would be much more dramatic.

Roland Hammond had been a social science
instructor at the college when I attended fifteen years earlier,
so I was familiar with him and his somewhat eccentric but

33

very knowledgeable skills as a teacher. I am not sure if he processed the difference in me, but I was a model student in the class and received the highest grade in the class. The awkwardness of being in my thirties and in the class with kids only slightly less than half my age would always be present for the next two years at the college and even more profound at the University of Alabama. However, being uncomfortable with my age overwhelmingly took back stage to my performance and accomplishment as a student. I was no longer content with being average and merely surviving academic obstacles. I developed a focus and determination to the extent of obsession at not only achieving an A in every class, but also having the highest grade in the class. Also, and very importantly, I took from every class something that I thought I would use when I started teaching. I made everything I learned relevant to my preparation for my future career. For the first time in my life, I felt I had a tremendous advantage over my fellow students in the classes. Certainly, the development of my prefrontal cortex helped me see more logically, but just as importantly, the real world of work, family, and spirituality provided me a great deal of valuable experience. I always sat on the front row in every class - even in the dozens of graduate classes following my bachelor's degree. I was the most outspoken in class discussions, and I set a very high bar in class presentations and projects for my fellow classmates. I think most of my classmates enjoyed my maturity and insights, but I am sure there were others who wondered why the old man in the class was causing such a commotion to the more traditional approach to attending college.

There are several points to make here about learning. My experiences working for A&P and on the farm taught me lessons about dealing with people who do not think and act as I do. I am afraid that most educators have been in school in some manner since early childhood and do not grasp the complexities in our society. Therefore, the multitude of family dynamics, learning styles, ability levels, behavioral issues, and regard for learning leave many educators unprepared at understanding and effectively responding to all the diversities. Nothing teaches more than experience, and my association with low income has shown me that breaking the cycle is possible. I have often had parents, students, and even teachers use poverty as an excuse for students performing and behaving badly. I have never accepted the excuse, and my personal experiences allow me to tell students and others that being poor is never a detriment to success - only a poor response to a lack of resources causes one to fail. For me, it was a determination to overcome that gave me strength and helped me to be successful.

It is also important to note that my mother's decision to associate me with people who cared about me and were models developed a strong desire on my part not to fail and disappoint those who were willing to invest in me. The family structure and function in our society has unquestionably changed in the last fifty years. In nearly every family where there are two parents, both must work. In increasing numbers, children are growing up in one-parent families. Far fewer families are involved in church and the activities there for children. The challenges and distractions to children in school are unprecedented, and there is less time and energy for parents to use in supporting and encouraging their children. As a result, it has become increasingly incumbent upon teachers and schools to prepare students for achievement and success. The encouragement, training, and motivation given to me by my family and church are no longer in place to a large and increasing extent, and schools are now often the only prominent positive factor in the lives of children - whether we like it or not. Educators now have an even more important role in investing in our children and our future.

Finally, what helped me to excel was the fact that I went back to school at a later age. Experience instilled in me a desire to work harder in order to be successful, but with maturity and personal development, I was able to see the connection between school and success. As educators, our good intentions at telling students how important school is must be replaced with demonstrations and modeling of the connection. Remember, the reasoning ability of students is not developed. Attempting to reason with children and students is most often futile. They will not listen. We must find a way to be more convincing in making education relevant to students if we are to make a successful investment.

Learning and Earning Interest

During my social studies undergraduate studies, I concentrated on political science and economics. My experience in business gave me some unique insights into economics. Based on my early interest in current political events, I became very interested in politics and government. The Kennedy assassination was my first meaningful exposure to government, and I became emotionally moved as I watched the events on black and white television. The reports laid a foundation for me on the basics of how the democracy in the United States functioned, as well as the nature of political responses from the media, Congress, and President Johnson. I struggle to explain how an eight-year-old child could be so engrossed in the events, but the mass attention to it all established an interest in the matters of state. I continued to focus on the functions of the government throughout the 1960s with the assassinations of Robert Kennedy and Martin Luther King Jr., the Vietnam War, and campus demonstrations against the war. About the only positive news item for me during the era was Apollo 11 landing on the moon on July 1969. As a first time presidential voter in 1972, I voted for Richard Nixon who won the election in a landslide. Then there was Watergate.

On June 17, 1972, the FBI investigating a burglary at the Democratic National Committee (DNC) headquarters at the Watergate Hotel found money on the burglars and traced it back to the Committee to re-elect the President. Later the U.S. Senate convened a bipartisan committee to investigate the possibility that the Nixon administration had been involved in the break in and possibly a subsequent cover-up. At every opportunity, and for hours on end, I watched the televised hearings with great interest as Sam Ervin, Howard Baker, and other members of the Senate questioned members of the administration, including Howard Dean and Alexander Butterfield who divulged the existence of White House tapes of Nixon meetings with his staff and others. The revelations moved Senator Baker to ask the famous question, "What did the President know, and when did he know it?" A series of breathtaking political incidences included the subpoenaing of the White House Tapes, a Supreme Court Case of *U.S. vs. Nixon*, and the ultimate resignation and removal from office of a standing president facing impeachment. The nation then faced the succession to the office of the presidency by a person who did not get a vote and finally the pardoning of a former president from all criminal charges. During the course of these events, I learned about stored information on Separation of Powers, Executive Privilege, the Supreme Court, and the U.S. Constitution. My knowledge about the workings of our government enhanced my interest in our government and economy. I continued to learn, and my interest increased with time as I read about and listened to relevant and real-life history in the making. It would all prove valuable to me when I entered the classroom.

What is Happening Here?

During my late twenties, something began happening to me as I concluded that I was not doing that for which I felt a calling. Investments were beginning to pay dividends as I gained a great deal of confidence in my ability and myself to handle difficult situations. I had gained valuable business experience, conquered the machinery disability, and could handle the machinery and farm work with any of the workers. My confidence had increased so much that I wanted to demonstrate that I could handle any task involving machinery. Therefore, in 1980 I decided that I wanted to fulfill a lifetime dream of mine to fly an airplane. I was fortunate in that my in-laws owned a Cessna 172 with four seats. My confidence became almost arrogance, and it is a wonder that I survived learning to fly an airplane.

After thirty hours of instruction and a solo flight with three landings, along with hours of studying for the written test, I climbed into the Cessna and began a one-hour flight to Birmingham International Airport. The moment I rotated off the runway, my flight instructor who also ran the airport called on the radio and asked if I was sure I wanted to make the flight. I assured him I was and told him that when I had contacted Flight Control, the agency confirmed the weather was clear five miles visibility. Anyone who lives east of the Mississippi River, especially those who fly, knows that haze is a major consideration for visual flight rules in the summer. I had flown into Birmingham at night with my instructor a few weeks earlier, and I was confident that it was no big deal. As I reached my cruising altitude, I became concerned because I could barely see the ground beneath me. My confidence and fear of failure made me continue the journey. I just could not see myself turning around and telling my instructor and my family that I had chickened out of the flight. At twenty miles out from the airport, I contacted approach control and reported my position and that I was inbound for landing. They responded with directions about heading and altitude and assigned me a transponder code.

As a rule, the approach at busy airports turn pilots over to the tower for final landing instructions at five miles out from the airport - when they confirm with the pilot that the airport is in sight. I was familiar with Birmingham from the ground, but when the controller radioed and asked if I had the airport in sight, I responded that I did not, and he directed me to inform him when I did. After a couple of minutes, I still did not have the runway in sight but radioed and told the controlled that I did when in fact I did not. All the time I was praying for the glimpse of my destination.

Finally, less than two miles out I saw the runway and began a fast descent, lowered my flaps, and made the landing, relieved and safely. I completed and passed the written test at the airport, got directions from the tower, and took off back home. I landed an hour later very proud that I had done well on the written test and passed, but mostly thankful that I had not killed myself. My instructor asked how the flight went, and I lied and informed him that it all went without incident.

I had apparently gone from having very little confidence to a somewhat reckless personality - something my wife has mentioned to me on several occasions. Reflecting on my career, there are probably some decisions and initiatives where I probably was a little too bold and should have exercised a little more caution. Despite my becoming a little reckless, adapting to machinery on the farm, becoming more competent in business skills, and learning to fly demonstrated my ability to set a goal and work hard to achieve the goal. I have to add that a great deal of my growth was the result of watching and learning from my father-in-law and his sons. I was constantly thinking and analyzing situations on the farm and in my family. When I did not understand something, I asked for an explanation. I wanted my children to be proud of me, and almost as important to my development, I wanted to be proud of myself. I listened, watched, asked questions, and learned. As a result, the investments made by many, along with my maturity, experience, and the development of my frontal cortex, or a combination of it all, I was finally at a major turning point in my life.

I was also realizing that farming or the business would not allow me to make the contribution I wanted to make in the world. Although I would become a full partner in the business, I always felt like an outsider who had married into the business. I was reasonably financially secure but felt I was always struggling for acceptance in the business with my partners and my young farmer friends. I tried as hard as I could for twelve years to become a businessperson and farmer, and I grew exponentially in knowledge and confidence. I just never felt I could be the man I wanted to be when I felt others believed I did not have to work in order to achieve success. My confidence had improved, but my self-image was still lacking. No matter how hard I tried and how much I overcame my propensity for failure, my talents were not in business or farming. There had to be some purpose in life for which I felt called. Even though people like my father-in-law can never understand that not everyone is good at what they feel portrays success, I believe that everyone has a calling for a career that utilizes their particular gifts and talents. I had the urge to be something other than the son-in-law of a man who would hand me success. I had to find myself and use any gift or talent God had given me. A person can force his or her way to be something that they are not, but true success only comes when we find our calling and follow the path intended for us to follow.

In education, we often prescribe teaching practices that attempt to provide the same learning for all students. I understand that high school does give students the opportunity to start to explore areas that may be of interest for a career. However, from kindergarten until graduation, we teach the core subjects of math, English, science, and social studies with the notion that each student should master the same things in each subject. The concept of everyone, no matter their talent or interest, attaining a level of proficiency in math, science, and language is our continued attachment of the assembly line concept of education. My father-in-law wanted everyone in the business to think and act in accordance with his philosophy. In education, we too often expect students to be what we want them to be, and often our investment offers very little opportunity for them to be the best at who and at what they are.

Learning to read is a good example. In my career, I have seen the emphasis in elementary education go from phonics to whole language instruction and back to phonics - two very different ends of the spectrum for reading instruction. Another way to teach reading, often mentioned but practiced too little, is morphology. Morphology is the study of base words with prefixes and suffixes that change or modify the meaning of the base words. A third methodology used in reading instruction is the ability of some children to identify sight words through memorization. I am convinced that each of these strategies can work and teach children to read. However, I do not think each strategy will work for all children. We often hear of blending reading instruction with every child exposed to the different strategies, but I propose that each child and teacher then identify and utilize the method that suits the child. Mountains of research and hundreds of products promote various methods and strategies to help students learn to read. Teachers and school systems spend millions of dollars trying to find the perfect product to produce good readers. The solution is not as elusive as we want to make it. Producing passionate students who can and want to read would solve many problems in education.

I personally do not understand phonics, and having me study letter sounds and mouth shapes is a waste of instructional time for me. My preferred method and the way I have determined that I learned to read is morphology. Morphology works for me but does not work for every child. Phonics and memorization do not work for every child. If I were an elementary teacher, I would have to avoid concluding that the way I learned to read is the best way for all children. Unfortunately, many teachers in every subject area utilize the methodology used to teach them as the method they use to teach students - because it worked for them.

To make reading instruction more effective, I propose grouping students based on his or her demonstration of what they understand and what works for them individually. Therefore, the classroom would have a group of phonics, sight word, morphology, and different combinations of the three reading strategies. If teachers teach reading with an assembly line mentality, with the teacher assuming that each child will learn a particular way, the results will be confused student readers and ultimately poorly performing students in all areas. The practice is what we refer to in education as differentiated instruction. In simple terms, the definition of differentiated instruction is using a different strategy of learning for each child based on his or her learning style. To me, the student learning style demonstrates the area for which the child is most gifted and interested. Yes, I said gifted. I believe that every child has a gift in some area. Our task as educators is to find that gifted area and reinforce, nurture, and foster it for each child. The assembly line approach to education attempts to clone learning and students and produce a product with similar skills and abilities that contradicts the concept that each child is different. Making learning interesting, meaningful, and relevant to the child's interest and ability requires a tremendous amount of effort and time from teachers. The easier and traditional form of instruction fails to maximize the tremendous potential achieved when students are actively engaged in true learning. To reiterate, we unfortunately expect students to be what we want them to be and not the best at whom and at what they are.

Theory to Practice

When I made the decision to return to school, I had to use every experience I had encountered in my life. My undergraduate training exposed me to a mountain of research on student learning and assessment of that

47

learning. I consider the preparation I received at the University of Alabama as the very best available. I was extremely fortunate to have been associated with many professors in my subject field who led me in the study of political science, geography, sociology, psychology, and human development. My studies in the College of Education gave me the tools to put into practice a method for delivery of the social sciences. Perhaps the best preparation for the classroom came from Dr. Patrick Ferguson in my social studies methodology class and the last education class I had prior to my internship. In his class, I learned to do lesson plans during the class and in the seven years in the classroom to follow, I would produce hundreds of daily lesson plans with behavioral objectives implemented into the lesson using a set, main body, and conclusion to the lesson. To this day, I can see the sheet of paper given to me with action verbs used in developing the objectives for the lesson. The task of students being able to demonstrate competency in lesson objectives required me to emphasize "how" and "what" the students were to learn. I still have the lesson unit of study I had to prepare for the class. My experience and preparation taught me to think about the big picture in instruction and to focus on concepts instead of basic knowledge and facts. I always introduced students to

Bloom's Taxonomy of Learning, and I always felt I was not doing justice to a lesson or the students if the instruction failed to include analysis, synthesis, and evaluation. Education seemed to abandon higher-order thinking and problem-solving strategies with the misguided emphasis of recall required to perform on the testing-based instruction dictated by the *No Child Left Behind Act*. Most educators are beginning to recognize the adverse outcomes of the act, and slowly progress is occurring to encourage more students to think and focus on depth of study. It is very interesting to me that what was encouraged twenty-five years ago has returned to a rightful place in learning methodology.

At the end of undergraduate methodology classes, teacher candidates began the important preparation from internship assignments. I had reminded my professors and advisors of my interest in government and economics, and the field placement office at the University responded with my assignment to Holt High School in a Government and Economics classroom. I was more than ready to find out if my experience, training, and commitment to teaching and learning would result in everything I had imagined and dreamed it would be. I was excited and a bit scared, but absolutely sure I was about to change the world of education - not unlike every teacher as his or her career begins. In some ways I would not be disappointed - in other ways I had only begun a learning experience for myself that would match any and all of the experiences I had prior to becoming a teacher. All the knowledge and experience I did have would be required to respond to the daily demands of being a teacher placed on me by the education system, but most of the demands I placed on myself. Looking back after twenty-five years, I realize I was not as prepared as I thought I was by any stretch of the imagination. Despite being older, more mature, and possessing a wealth of experiences, I would still have so much to learn. It is difficult to imagine how my daughter and other young teachers, who lack the qualities and advantages I had, are able to cope with the demands associated with teaching and managing a classroom. As we consider ways to improve education, a good step would be to develop and invest in mentoring programs or internships that are more meaningful and productive for beginning teachers. Just as importantly, educators must realize that many students do not acclimate to learning as well as others. Students and teachers need strong mentoring services in order for our education system to move from being just good enough to being great.

Sally was an institution at the high school where I participated in the internship program. She was one of the very first black teachers hired by the system and had been at the school since 1970 when the system became fully integrated. She was very active in the Alabama Education Association and the Democratic Party at the state and national levels. In fact, she had attended two Democratic National Conventions as a delegate. Politically, we were worlds apart. However, her intense personality and especially her sense of humor made my association with her for three months enjoyable, and we never had any disagreements. Sally was at the point in her career when nothing seemed to stress her, and so she came across as somewhat laid back regarding almost everything except for her beloved Democratic Party. It was 1989, the interest and planning for the 1992 presidential race was beginning to develop, and Sally was working to make sure Bill Clinton got the White House. I was as pumped as any new teacher and anxious to begin my journey in education. We talked about plans for the semester, and it became clear to me that Sally was fine with me taking as much control of her four American Government classes and one advanced ninth grade geography class as I wanted. Of course, I wanted it all. In effect, she gave me the responsibility for all the classes and told me she would be available if I needed her.

Almost immediately, I was popular with the students, even though my first day in front of the class I had left an opened highlighter in my shirt pocket and developed a huge yellow spot on my white and blue pinstriped shirt. Except for a few brief clinical placements in undergraduate classes, I was experiencing my first real association with high school kids in seventeen years. I noticed very quickly that the school culture had changed since my time in high school. However, the change was slight compared to the changes I would see for the next twenty-seven years. The most apparent change was with the girls in the classes. During the seventies, girls were usually reserved and did not participate in many of the antics in which boys participated. As a teacher and an administrator, I learned that I could not have "rabbit ears" when around high school students. Teachers often have to ignore things that are overheard. I ignored many comments in my internship. I heard girls talking about attendance at wild parties on the weekend, how they avoided their parents when arriving back home, and numerous other activities involving questionable conduct. In 1989, the girls were now part of the antics that my male friends and I participated in during high school that the girls usually avoided.

I was thirty-five years old and in a middle-class school environment, yet many of the girls thought I was the coolest person at the school. I was very embarrassed when I overheard comments concerning my dress, hair, and general appearance as I walked among the students in the classes. As a teacher and administrator, I have witnessed and had to deal with several unfortunate instances of inappropriate conduct between teachers and students. I know several individuals with careers cut short by certain inappropriate actions of the teacher. I am thankful that I was older when I started in schools and that I had a moral base that prompted me to always keep a wall between the students and me. I can honestly say without hesitation that I have never participated in any conduct in any way inappropriate with any student. Over the years, as I have talked to young teachers I hired or spoke with in college groups, I have warned them of the pitfalls that can destroy their career and reputation, including inappropriate relationships with students. During my days as a teacher and principal, the issues were always with male teachers and female students. Nowadays, it seems that a majority of the inappropriate instances involve female teachers and male students. Things are still changing.

I did discover immediately, and the revelation has stuck with me throughout the years, that students enjoy being challenged and that they desire structured and engaging instruction. Since the students in my internship were mine from the beginning of the year, they accepted the demands I made on learning and were eager to please me. This would not be the case in my first real job that started in the middle of the school year. In return for their enthusiasm, I progressively felt a strong obligation to provide opportunities for them to think, problem-solve, and learn. Their expectations motivated me to plan well and work hard. I felt in each class that I was on stage and that others were judging me by my performance as a teacher. We developed a relationship in which the students expected much of me just as I expected much of them. I tried to model what I expected from them by demonstrating my passion for the subject, as well a desire for them to question and think. I posed provoking questions in class for which there were very few quick or absolute answers. The atmosphere was intoxicating, and the students developed a sense of security and confidence that allowed them to ask questions and to challenge my assertions and explanations of how government and the economy worked. Every day was exciting and rewarding for me, and I wanted to make sure it was for every student also.

Up until I gave my first exam, I was convinced the students were learning the material and enjoying the lessons and that I was perhaps the best teacher I knew. As it turned out, they were only enjoying the lessons. It was obvious that students lacked exposure to the kind of assessments that reflected the thought-provoking instruction, even though active learning was taking place in my classroom. I still believe this is a problem in schools today. There has been tremendous emphasis in the last few years on instructional methodologies as a pathway for students to perform well on standardized achievement tests. However, most teachers are not very well equipped to create assessments similar to questions confronting students on achievement tests. It reminds me of football teams that look very good on the practice fields as they go through drills and run the offense and defense against teammates with less experience and ability. However, those football players may not look so good in a live scrimmage against good players or other teams on game day. Even NFL teams play pre-season games to find out just how good the team is against real foes. In order for students to perform well on standardized assessments, they need continual exposure to challenging classroom assessments that reflect the same structure and reasoning found on the more formal gauges of achievement. As much as I had to work on challenging students with daily higher-order thinking in the lessons, I had to exert almost as much energy on preparing tests that would require the same skills. My responsibilities for student learning increased dramatically as I looked for ways to improve student test-taking skills and their confidence at addressing questions without obvious right answers. I had to develop and implement assessment strategies to match high-level instruction, and more importantly, teach the students how to use the same skills on tests they engaged in during lessons.

I also made another startling discovery. Students could but would not write! As I mentioned in chapter 1, students wanted to just choose an answer and move on. Multiple-choice, matching, and fill-in-the-blank questions that the students were most accustomed to and comfortable with required little thinking, and if all else failed, a simple guess would work. I was amazed and disappointed at how quickly the students, with a little thought or considering other alternatives, took a shot at answering what I considered well-constructed multiple-choice questions. However, the short answer, table and graph interpretations, and essays were not even worth the effort, and a majority of the students did not even attempt to answer. Considering that I was working with high school seniors, many of whom would be applying for college, I was beyond shocked and sick with frustration.

I reported to Sally the results from my first exam and that I was sure I could help students at utilizing higher-order skills in dealing with the multiple-choice sections of my tests, but I was at a loss on the writing skills and was at a point of simply giving up. The students were in twelfth grade, and if they did not have the ability to write by now, how could they ever? Students first begin writing paragraphs in the second grade. In my experience in elementary school and school review visits, I have seen the sample paragraphs on boards and powerpoints and heard the discussions of topic sentences, supporting statements, and concluding statements. Unfortunately, I have seen the same demonstrations in eleventh grade English classrooms. Something is apparently not working. If students are writing paragraphs in second grade, why do we still have to teach the exact same thing in eleventh grade? I am afraid that as far as writing is concerned, English teachers are doing the same things regardless of the grade level and most social studies, science, and math teachers feel that writing is taught in English, and most of them avoid writing assessments altogether. Sally suggested I visit the Advanced Placement English teacher for advice on teaching writing. This would be my first encounter with AP, the program that would later prove to be the most rewarding experience of my teaching career. Visiting the English teacher would also begin a journey in a process, including dozens of improvements and revisions for writing in social studies that would be a focal point in my teaching career.

THREE

Sue was a typical English teacher with impeccable speech, grammar, and language skills. In her presence, and in the presence of almost all English teachers, I feel a sense of caution about saying something grammatically incorrect. It is a feeling not unlike the feeling I have with a medical doctor, lawyer, or banker. I suppose this comes from my modest and insecure childhood. Today, I play golf regularly with doctor and banker friends of mine and have no issues with them or other professionals on the golf course. It does remain an issue when I visit other doctors and professionals in their offices. Interestingly, my daughter is an English teacher. More interesting, I am now married to the best English teacher I have ever known – without intimidation.

Experimental Teaching

Sue introduced me to a one-page outline for a five-paragraph mini-thesis paper and suggested that I use it to work with my students. The one page would eventually become a series of outlines, examples, and rubrics. The students in my advanced class were also in her AP class, and Sue and I would both be teaching the same structure. There is a novel idea - cross-curricular collaboration. I assumed incorrectly that she used it in her regular English classes. Happy that I had had the discussion with Sue, I now had a tool to give to the students what I was sure would enlighten them and solve all the writing problems. I was a bit reckless and presumptive in my diagnosis of the problem and the simple solution I thought I had found. After making copies of the one-page instructions and going over it with the students, I felt confident that they could now at least write a paragraph with a topic sentence, supporting statements, and a concluding sentence. I even allowed the students to use the instructions and gave them a simple topic. I guess it would be like Charles Lindbergh saying he had a plan and would simply jump into the plane fly to Paris. The solution was not that simple, and the papers were again a disaster. Once again, we started over.

Even though I had been discouraged and disappointed, my determination stepped in, and I vowed to teach the kids to write. Upon entering the classroom on what would be the first of a three-day sabbatical from the structure and function of American Government, students saw a table at the front of the class with a loaf of bread, a plastic knife, and a jar of peanut butter. They obviously had no clue of what I was up to, but they knew me well enough already to know it was something very different. Every class that day had similar procedures and results. I asked a volunteer to sit in the chair facing the students and in front of the table with my bread and peanut butter. All eyes in the room were on the demonstration as I announced that we were going to make a peanut butter sandwich. The catch was that the volunteer would provide specific directions to me in order to make the sandwich. During the course of the day, I had torn open the bread, stuck my hand into the jar of peanut butter, put peanut butter on almost everything on or around the table, made a huge mess, and ruined another perfectly good shirt. After each demonstration, we discussed the point of such a misuse of food. Using probing and guiding questions, we came to several conclusions and related them to writing. Students saw the need to be specific, descriptive, methodical, and concise. Most of all they learned to develop a mental picture of what they were saying and what the reader would envision from what they were writing. Later, as I graded papers and there were arguments or descriptions that lacked clarity or proof, I only labeled the portion as PB, and every student knew what that meant.

As we discussed and practiced examples of thesis statements, I used example after example of how to use academic arguments in writing. I referred to media editorials, doctoral dissertations, and arguments by attorneys in a courtroom setting. Finally, I gave the students a topic, and they developed their own thesis statement from the topic. They also learned about how the thesis statement was the last statement in the introductory paragraph and the first sentence in the last. I often told the students it was almost biblical that the first is last and the last is first. The students created their thesis argument, and we were ready for research. The biggest difficulty for the students was avoiding a narrative approach to their writing or simply writing a report. It was obvious that the only writing the students had done was using these approaches, and neither of the styles required them to reason and think of arguments to support their thesis. We had to move from just saying what others said to using what others said to support our ideas. It was always a constant struggle to encourage the students to take a stand and to support it with documented evidence. I had to get back to American Government, so I proposed that any student needing more assistance could meet with me at the public library after school, and I would continue to provide individual help. I expected a dozen students to show up, but sixty-five students showed up after school. When we left that evening, I had worked with every student in developing their three arguments for the body of the paper and directed them to possible research to use in the paper.

The students in my intern classes would write two papers for me during my time with them. Amazingly, everyone turned a paper in and nearly everyone had made an acceptable grade. For those who did not perform well enough to get a passing grade, I gave the paper back and had them correct the paper using the ideas and suggestions I gave them. Years later, as a principal, I would develop and implement a school strategy that required students who did not perform well on any assignment to redo the assignment. Eventually, all the students passed, and I placed all the best papers on the bulletin board. For days, the students came into the room and stared at the wall covered with papers that received an *A*. Others said their paper would be on the wall next time. Many of the students had never experienced any academic success, much less had their work posted on the wall for all to see. I used the same approach for seven years in the classroom with the same results with every paper written. During my years in the classroom, students wrote a paper during every grading period, usually resistant and grumbling at the beginning but actually anxious to write more after the first one. I have had many students come back to me and thank me for teaching them to write. My investment of time and effort in teaching students to write was paying dividends.

I could have given up many times during the initial writing activity. I spent hours preparing, teaching, re-teaching, motivating, encouraging, and always referring to the project even in our daily lessons. The results proved to me that students do what we expect of them. I also confirmed that writing is an instrument that demonstrates learning and requires thinking and reasoning. The essence of all learning is for students to think, utilize creativity, plan, develop, and articulate. To me, writing requires all of these components.

It is important to note that during my internship, Dr. Joyce Sellers, the principal at the school who was later appointed the district superintendent, would become a mentor for me when I began my career in administration.

She would have a profound effect on me personally and on my career. She told me later that I was the only intern she had ever had in a school that had students in her office crying and begging her to hire me for the good of the school.

I learned during my student teaching that in spite of my maturity, confidence, and success, I still had much to learn. It was reassuring to me that I did have success, and I will never forget the students. I hope that I left some impression on each of them. One student in particular was very special. Roman was a natural leader and the quarterback on the football team, debate captain, and a model student. He has continued to be successful and is now a practicing attorney in town.

My home had burned to the ground two years earlier while I was in undergraduate school. We lost everything except for the clothes we had with us at the beach. My church family, neighbors, friends, and a few complete strangers gave us money and household items. The church also had a shower for us and the congregation overwhelmed us with generosity and kindness. Just before my time ended for my internship, Roman's house burned down, and I gave him $50 and told him of my experience. Years later, I ran into him, and he recalled my showing up at a football game and then meeting each player and congratulating them on a big win as they came off the field. He talked about all we had learned together, but he said the money I gave him had been one of the most memorable experiences that he recalled. He expressed the same gratitude for the gift as I felt only a few years before from those who had done the same for me.

All the students were wonderful, and we had a big party on my last day at the school. They had provided me with hope as an educator and in young people, which was contingent upon parents, teachers, and the community providing them with the opportunity and encouragement to succeed. High school had changed a great deal from the time I had graduated, but the differences were very subtle compared to the changes that would occur over the next eleven years when I would return to the same school as the principal.

Practice to Practice

My Director of Human Resources office window looks out at one of the business highways in our area. I have always gotten to work early, usually by 6:30 A.M. when the official day starts at 8:00. I have found that my quiet time provides the peace I need to prepare myself for what are normally active days. That is less true now than when I was a teacher and even more so when I was a school principal. It is amazing how much can be accomplished in an hour and a half of uninterrupted time. Most mornings I have time for another cup of coffee, and as I look out the window at all the traffic, I often ponder the destinations of the travelers and their attitudes about their jobs and responsibilities for the day. As the Human Resource Director, I often have the responsibility of dealing with employees with a variety of issues that often interfere with the effective performance of their jobs. As a young boy, listening to my mom and dad and their complaints and unhappiness with their jobs, watching the workers for my grandfather, working with disgruntled people at the A&P and on the farm, and dealing with teachers and support personnel who do not like their jobs, I realize how fortunate I am to have found my place. I truly love coming to work each day. I often wonder what percentage of the people on the highway hate going to work. How many are trying to perform their job lacking passion and enthusiasm? How many people look at their job as only a way to make a living? I can empathize with their attitude since I have been in their place. I am blessed and very fortunate to have had the opportunity to go back to school, change careers, and find my place. At the end of my internship, I was ready to confirm that my career change would in fact bring me happiness and fulfill my desire to follow the path meant for me.

I had begun the application process with all the area school systems while finishing my internship. However, finishing in December severely limited the opportunities I had for interviews. I did interview with the Personnel Director for the Tuscaloosa County School System. Dr. Hinton was a veteran human resources person, and I developed a very good relationship with him over the next several years. I learned much about personnel from my association with him and refer to him often as my mentor for my current position. I also had the pleasure of teaching his son who was one of the brightest students I had the pleasure of teaching. Dr. Hinton was encouraging but offered no indication of any current employment possibilities or any in the near future. Such is the practice of any good human resource person. For the first time since going back to school, I was a little discouraged, but I did have a plan.

I knew that my undergraduate degree was not where I wanted to end my education. I loved college and I loved learning. Therefore, I began the enrollment process in graduate school at the University of Alabama. One evening, relatively late, I got a phone call from Dr. Hinton. A Tuscaloosa County Board Meeting had just ended, and he informed me that a government and economics teacher at Tuscaloosa County High transferred to an assistant principal's position at another high school. He instructed me to call the principal immediately and tell him Dr. Hinton said to call about the position. I was nervous as I could be. It was nine o'clock at night, and I was concerned about calling a principal so late in the evening. It turns out that my fear was justified.

Mr. Walker answered the phone and sounded as if I had gotten him up and out of bed. I told him of my instructions to call him about the social studies position at his school. Apparently, he had not attended the meeting and said he knew nothing about an opening. He grumbled something about Dr. Hinton and told me he guessed he could see me at 9:00 A.M. in two days. I hung up the phone shaken and fearing that I had destroyed any chance for the position. I found out later that the principal's wife was extremely ill, which only added to his bad first impression of me. Nevertheless, determined to give it my best shot, I prepared myself for the interview. The position was the perfect job I had prayed for - teaching my favorite areas of government and economics.

Two days later I arrived at the school all dressed up in my best suit with my intern unit in hand. I was nervous again but more about meeting the principal with the gravelly voice that made me think of Coach Bryant. After a greeting form a very nice secretary, I told her I had an appointment for an interview. She left the office, went down the little hall, and came back with a man who introduced himself as the assistant principal and told me to follow him. Down the little hall, we made right turn into a very large and well-furnished office with stuffed flying Mallard ducks on the wall. All I remember were the ducks, but I am sure there were other pictures on the walls. Sitting at his desk was Bobby Walker, a Bear Bryant lookalike who would remind me following the interview of my father-in-law with his no-nonsense, stoic, and businesslike personality. He introduced me to both assistants, both of whom would be principals at the school later. We commenced with a laid back and informal inquiry into my experiences, who we may have known mutually, and a great deal about farming. The assistant principals asked most of the questions that dealt mostly with management and discipline issues. Mr. Walker listened and made some follow up interjections from time to time. After about forty-five minutes, the three looked at each other and asked if I had any questions. I think that may be when I asked about the ducks on the wall.

Mr. Walker remarked to the assistants that he had heard enough and that as far as he was concerned, I was the man for the job. My face must have been beaming with excitement as both assistants said they were satisfied that I would be perfect for the class. I put the ducks out of my head. Mr. Walker got on the phone and called Dr. Hinton at the central office. I heard him tell Hinton that they had found their man and that he wanted me as his new teacher. Keep in mind this was only two days after the board had approved a promotion of the former teacher, without properly announcing, posting, and interviewing other candidates for the position. I could only hear one side of the conversation, but Dr. Hinton must have brought up points about postings, board approvals, and needing to interview other possible candidates - none of which I knew anything about at the time. I did not know all the legal formalities I now know, but I was still relieved when I heard Mr. Walker say that he really didn't care - this is who I want! Walker said okay, hung up the phone, and made some disparaging remark regarding Dr. Hinton. I am sure they were not best friends. He did inform me that I would not officially start until after the board meeting, but asked if I would be interested in coming to the school and spending a little time with the outgoing teacher and his students before he left. I enthusiastically agreed to another serious personnel error by today's litigious workplace standards.

Teach Me to Fish

Ironically, the most popular teachers in schools are either the most laid back and less demanding or those who set high standards and expect nothing but the best from their students. I have often warned young teachers in groups and individually that trying to be popular with students the incorrect way will most often contribute to negative circumstances down the road. I have also determined that there is a huge difference between popularity and respect. Popularity does not guarantee respect, but respect most often produces popularity. The teacher I was replacing in the middle of the school year was popular with the students. What I had witnessed in the few days I visited the class was that the teacher was making the students very comfortable. The routine that was followed on a daily basis provided no surprises, little anticipation, and only passive engagement. Ellen A. Skinner and Michael J. Belmont determined in 1993 that there are reciprocal effects in a classroom between the teacher and students regarding productive engagement and learning.

Four possible classroom environments exist that can determine the engagement of the teacher and the students. The least effective situation in a classroom is passive-passive, in which neither the teacher nor the students are in any way engaged in teaching and learning. In a passive-passive classroom, the teacher is most often sitting at his/her desk and either working on grading papers, checking emails, or working on other tasks not related to the lesson. Sometimes teachers engage in athletic plans or plays, fundraising, or other extracurricular endeavors. Too many times, there are video presentations on the television or projection screen. Incidentally, I will mention that some of the videos I have observed in my career have not even remotely related to the curriculum. The students in passive-passive classrooms watch videos, work on dubious assignments, copy notes off the board, read, talk, and even sleep. As a principal, I got occasional complaints from parents and students, but most often everyone was content and the teacher was popular because there were such low expectations. Unless there happened to be a bad grade report for a student, everyone was happy. The usual response from the student about a bad grade was to sell out the teacher, proclaiming hardly ever was anything done in the class or the teacher did not teach. Although popular, passive teachers gain little respect, and there is little loyalty from students. Often the bad grade was the result of a behavioral issue or not completing a minimum amount of the assignments - what we often refer to as "busy work." The damage done to student achievement in a passive-passive environment is severe and illustrates incompetency on the part of the teacher.

Active-passive is a second type of engagement in a classroom, where a well-meaning teacher works hard presenting information to the students and making sure all the objectives and standards are covered. However, the students usually ignore the active teacher's efforts. For a multitude of reasons, the students passively participate by not being involved in any thinking, problem solving, or other creative endeavors. Students simply follow directions and little more. Often the active teacher plans activities that involve the students and attempts to elicit higher-order reasoning and thinking, but somehow a connection fails between the teacher and the students. The lack of student engagement may be the result of a teacher's lack of personality, charisma, sense of humor, attractiveness, flexibility, or a complicated mixture of all these elements. Active teachers with passive students are not very popular with students, and any respect is more out of fear of a bad grade than appreciation for the hard work of the teacher.

Interestingly, some students perform well in an active-passive environment. As I mentioned earlier, some students just want information they can recall for the class exam, and some may even be able to infer a few concepts, get a good grade, and move on. Just give me the answers - please.

A third type of engagement in classrooms is passive-active. Much of the current emphasis in teaching methodologies is for teachers to act as facilitators and to empower students to be active learners. Generally, the passive-active classroom may seem to be in unison with research that indicates students learn best from each other. However, passive teaching is not the same as student-centered teaching. In a true and effective student-centered environment, there is a tremendous amount of teacher activity and planning that sets up the instructional period for active student engagement. Merely assigning large amounts of seatwork, homework, assignments without proper structure and parameters, and assessments without enumerated expectations of outcomes can be a disguise for student-centered instruction and only be a passive-active classroom. I have observed as a principal that these types of classroom structures produce the most complaints from students and parents because of the lack structure and directions provided to the students by the teachers. In effect, the passive-active classroom exists where the teacher invests little and expects a great deal. The fourth type of classroom structure illustrates true student-centered instruction.

An active-active classroom is one facilitated by the teacher who plans, reflects, provides structure, and assesses on a continual basis in order for students to analyze, create, problem-solve, question, and learn through collaboration with other students with little interference from the teacher. The actual planning by the teacher takes hours outside the classroom, during the summer, and during breaks in the school calendar. Active-active classroom teachers do not go home at the end of the day and not think about school until the next day. They constantly monitor student progress and provide guidance and motivation to students individually during the instructional period. The active teacher is constantly looking for ways to invest in student learning by focusing on depth of knowledge and helping students grasp concepts, ask questions, and communicate learning. Active-active classrooms prepare students to be lifelong learners. The active teacher invests in students and the profession and recognizes that dividends from the investments are students with confidence and skills necessary to be successful in life, regardless of the path the student may take.

The teacher I replaced was passive concerning academics and very active about management and discipline. He was a law and order man in every sense of the word. Students in the class daily faced simple procedures and predictable outcomes. A good grade in the class resulted from proper behavior along with exhibiting responsibility in fulfilling the rather trivial assignments in a timely manner. The respect the students had for the teacher resulted from his legalistic fairness, predictability, and reputation for order. In his class, following his rules made good grades easy to achieve. The teacher proclaimed to me that his way was the only way and that it was in my best interest to follow his example. The students understood his game and jumped through the necessary hoops in order to take another step toward graduation without a great deal of effort. The students were very good at playing his game.

Run the Reverse

The fact that I am a native Alabamian and a graduate of the University of Alabama, it would be a gross understatement to say I am fond of football. The Crimson Tide has not won so many games and national titles by deception or tricks. The team has always taken to "manning up" and physically challenging the opposition. In close games, I often catch myself being sometimes frustrated with the conservative nature of the play calling. I want to see the coaches and players getting the opposing team thinking and moving one way and then to run a reverse play in the opposite direction. After I spent a few days with the departing teacher, and after observing the mundane class procedures, I knew I was going to have to pull a reverse out of my bag. However, I did not foresee the reaction I would get from the students when lecture notes were not on the overhead transparency device when they came into the room. Many asked what was going on, and some just sat gazing at the blank screen at the front of the room and thinking that they would possibly have to do nothing in class. The game was about to change, and I would turn the students' academic world upside down.

The most important characteristic of successful teachers is the passion they have for sharing with others the love they have for their subjects. As a human resource director, I have the opportunity to travel to colleges and universities in the state to meet and do brief interviews with prospective teachers for our system. During the recruiting interviews, as well as the interviews I did when hiring teachers when I was a principal, I always seek to determine a level of passion from the student about his or her major. I usually ask why they chose the particular area of study for a major. I am always listening for a student to refer to a calling or being on a mission to teach others what they love so much. It is vitally important to me for teachers to believe and communicate that what they teach is the most important subject students can learn. A teacher with the passion I look for inevitably considers the subject they teach as the area most important to the future success of students - regardless of the career the student may pursue.

The combination of all my experiences, along with the investments of so many people who counseled and encouraged me, instilled in me a passion for teaching and a desire to make a difference in as many young people as I could. I was now at the point where I could begin to invest in students through my hard work, dedication, and determination to be an influential teacher and role model. My confidence was secure, yet I still had what I refer to as a healthy fear of failure. What I had seen in clinical experiences and during my internship, as well as what I had witnessed in various employment and personal experiences, developed in me a wide angle view of education and a rather dramatic opinion about changes I wanted to attempt to make during my career. The vision has stayed with me in every position I have held and remains today.

I arrived for my first day at Tuscaloosa County High School as an official teacher at 6:30 A.M. on January 21, 1990. I was still living forty-five miles away in Fayette County, so I had to leave the house at 5:30 each day. I had commuted from Fayette to the University and my internship for two years, so the trip was nothing new for me. I had found that during the commute I often had time to reflect and think during the drive through the rural countryside of West Alabama. Now the commute to work each day offered me the same peace and opportunity for a great amount of reflection and planning. I recall that I was anxious to get started but not necessarily nervous. After my experience in my internship, I was confident for the same reaction from the students and staff. The former teacher was out the door, and the classes were now mine. We were going to do some learning.

TCHS, built in 1926, had served generations of students. It was the school where the wife of Governor George Wallace and Alabama's only woman governor, Lurleen B. Wallace graduated from high school. My room was upstairs in the first of two additions added to the school after 1926. The former occupant of the room had done nothing to enhance the appeal of the room. The desks were all in rows, and chalk dust covered every exposed surface in the room. The dust in every corner and on every unused surface made it obvious that the room had gone without cleaning for years. For several weeks, before and after school, I dusted and cleaned every square inch of the room and cleaned out a closet with books, papers, and everything else that the teacher had accumulated over several years. I cleaned and disinfected every desk and chair, but the graffiti written on the furniture and the gum pasted underneath were there in infamy. I often walked around the room during my prep period when students were not in the room and read some of the names and messages written on the tops of the desks. Since I once found a desk at the University with Kenny "Snake" Stabler's name carved into it, I was hoping I might find where Lurleen Wallace had signed a desk. Mrs. Wallace must have been a student before my room existed or she had objections to defacing public property. I also thought reading some of the messages could provide me with some insight and help in getting into the heads of the students and having a better understanding of them. I decided I did not want to get into students' heads based on many of the writings I read.

It was obviously clear to me that in order to institute change and to start doing the things I wanted to do with the classes, I first had to put to a stop many of the things the students were doing. As I mentioned, the students were very comfortable with the simple expectations for success in the class. They knew what to expect each day when they walked into the room. Clear, practiced, and reinforced procedures became ritualistic. My first step would be to dismiss common procedure that did little to promote student achievement. As simple as it may seem, the classroom arrangement has a great deal to do with the atmosphere in a classroom. Desks in rows arranged in straight lines reinforce traditional views of order, organization, and efficiency but prevent discussion and the sharing of thoughts and ideas. Looking people in the eye is essential for effective communication. Looking at the back of the heads of others in the class prohibited the type of dialogue I wanted for the class. It was also an obstacle for me to be able to navigate the room in order to establish personal contact with individual students. Following the first day of class, and every day thereafter for the remainder of my teaching career, students sat in a u-shape arrangement and had to look others in the eye across the aisle. They would also have to adjust to my standing and working in their space. It was like standing outside when suddenly a massive shower drenches a group of people when my students arrived in class the following day of class. Questions and concerns came from all directions. Why are the desks like this? Where am I supposed to sit? Who did this? Will the desks stay this way?

The second procedure to stop was the projection of notes on the projector screen. During my career, I have witnessed this procedure many times. It does prevent the teacher from having to repeat important information and eliminates the possibility of students missing something they may see again on a test, but it does not require a very important component associated with an active classroom - listening. Perhaps the teacher who resorts to giving students information for the test is the result of giving up on engaging students and keeping their attention. Maybe it is just easier on everyone involved to have a full course outline of notes amassed on a roller and scrolled up each day for the students to copy down in their notebooks. Next year the teacher simply pulls out the roller and here we go again. One of the biggest obstacles I would have to overcome was the expectation of students to be spoon-fed information. So many times a discussion was taking place in my room when suddenly we would discover a concept of revelation, and I would explode with enthusiasm over the discovery, only to look at the students listening but not writing a word down. I reiterated the importance, at which point the pens and pencils took off like the start of a NASCAR race at Talladega Motor Speedway. My students required and received intensive training to listen, but they also had to learn to manage and store information gleaned from various activities in the classroom. A big part of my responsibility was to teach students how to learn. No longer would students be shoveled information.

My third period class was the largest and perhaps most active class I had during my first semester at TCHS. Like the students in all the classes, they had a very bad case of senioritis; however, this group seemed to be the most vocal about just getting high school completed. The class started each day at 10:00, the time that most teenagers actually wake up. There is even research that indicates we would be better starting classes in high school in mid-morning and continuing until early evening. However, our goal in education has always been to have students come to us rather than us going to them. Getting back to my point, somewhere around ten minutes before class was over in third period, half the class got up and headed to the door. I asked what was happening and was informed by the one of the obvious leaders of the class that the former teacher had allowed the students who co-oped (had jobs and went to school) to get a jump on other students and exit the school. The students left provided they had completed copying all the notes and finishing any other assignment for the day. I was stunned as they walked out the door. I checked with the administration at the school to make sure I would not be violating any policy or procedure in stopping the process. I found out there was no such regulation. It was a way the teacher had motivated the students to hurry and finish each day. The next day I announced the practice would stop and that our time in class would start and end at the bell. You would think I had announced the legal driving age was changing to age eighteen based on the student's reaction my doing away with the practice.

The final and most difficult change would involve the well-overdone practice of class worksheets. Simple and short answers with no thinking required were the hallmark of most social studies classes at the time. We had discussed the misuse of the devices in my methodology classes, and I had witnessed the massive scale of the practice in my brief experiences in classrooms and with my own children. Using handouts occupies students during class and provides them with opportunities for easy grades. Teachers used them extensively, and students loved them and expected at least one a day in every class.

Teaching accessories accompany textbooks and are the tools that often persuade teachers to adopt a particular textbook. Textbook companies make literally billions of dollars from the book sales and these supplemental products, and there is tremendous competition among book publishers based on the quantity of teacher material that come with the book. Notice that I said *teacher* versus *teaching* materials. Included in the materials were worksheets or workbooks that go along with the textbook and include questions related to the information found in the book. Most often, the sheets consist of multiple choice, short answer, fill-in-the blank, and true-false questions that for the most part require the student to look for bold-faced words in the passages. Most have a feeble final attempt at summarizing some obscure concept the students may be able to infer from the reading. The worksheets have long been the source of daily assignments in the classroom, used for daily grades, and averaged with the chapter tests, also provided with the teacher materials. All too often, some teachers become clerical workers as they copy, distribute, and grade the work. I have even seen teachers who required the students to answer the worksheets on a separate sheet of paper in order to file the materials and use them year after year until the next book adoption took place - usually around five years. My students were used to, expected, and even demanded the worksheets in order to get the daily grade that would offset the bad score they would inevitably receive on the forthcoming test. The worksheets and extra credit opportunities, along with a much too common "participation" grade were all a part of the game played in the classroom. Removing these avenues for a passing grade from the students in my classroom created a great deal of disequilibrium among my students who were in the middle of their senior year in high school.

There is a common mentality in education that the next and latest product or program, along with the proper teacher training, which most always accompanies the product, will revolutionize and reform teaching and learning. During my career, the number of programs and products and the millions of dollars used to purchase the materials is staggering, and any positive effects are at the very least questionable. The effect has been the atomization of education and in particular instruction. Fourteen clubs is the limit of golf clubs a golfer can have in his golf bag. I do not know exactly the reasoning for the rule, but as confused as I get with fourteen options, I can only imagine how complicated the next shot would be if I had say twenty-eight choices. I submit that educators may have too many clubs in the bag, and the result is that we become confused and indecisive about what and when to use a particular program or product. Perhaps it is time to start looking at all our programs and removing things and abandoning the practice of consistently adding and never taking away things that may not be effective.

For example, I recently heard a presentation from some administrators from another system talking about formative assessments they use. During the discussion, the presenters stated that there was little or no correlation between the purchased formative assessment tool and the end-of-the-year achievement test used to determine the state academic status of the school. The question I asked at the end of the presentation was if there was no correlation, why waste the money and instructional time? The only answer I could get was that the formative assessment was used prior to the new achievement test was required, and the system had never stopped using it. If we want education reform that is effective, we have to consider it is time to start eliminating things we do not find helpful before we ever invest in anything else we hope will be useful. We also have to do our best to make sure any new investment pays dividends in the form of improved student achievement. We should not chase every rabbit that comes along into a hole.

Instituting all these changes requires a tremendous amount of time and energy on my part. Dealing with substantial resistance for change from the students consumed a great deal of my time and energy. Gone was the easy way to a good grade. The reverse had been called, and we were about to run it.

On Second Thought, Just Give me the Fish

I display my three college diplomas and other awards and recognitions in my office like many other professionals. Each plaque represents accomplishments of which I am very proud. What is most important about the items on the wall is not necessarily the accomplishment but the work and commitment that produced them. All that I have and anything I may have accomplished in my life came as a result of sacrifice, commitment, and perseverance. Nothing has ever come easily. My struggles in childhood with poverty and an alcoholic and mostly-absent father required a determination to overcome. Every fear, along with the challenges associated with low self-esteem and lack of confidence were obstacles that stood between success and me. The journey in overcoming has made me strong, and I am thankful for every opportunity I have had to avoid failure by remaining steadfast in my desire to be successful. I do not feel unique in my journey, and I have observed that almost all people succeed as a result of hard work and strong-willed determination - along with the investment from others.

Athletics again offers a good example of everything coming with a cost. I have been associated with dozens of raw-talented young men and women who displayed extraordinary ability who never were able to be successful because they failed to develop the skills necessary to produce results. Jumping high, running fast, and being strong does not equate to exceptional performance unless those abilities are refined and developed by a tremendous amount of hard work aimed at a goal to succeed. Every All-American athlete and his or her coach, from gymnastics to football, recognize that dedication and years of hard work produce excellence. Like me, almost everyone at some point has a vision for what each wants to accomplish in life. For many, when roadblocks or obstacles appear, there develops a challenge to the commitment, the vision fades, and many abandon the dream. Individuals often lack the determination and fortitude to overcome setbacks. I have been fortunate to have been blessed with many who encouraged and invested in me, but I also know that along with fortune and help, what has made me successful in my career has been my hard work and determination.

Based on my success in my internship, I carried with me considerable enthusiasm and confidence to my new job. Little did I know that all the preparation I had been through, along with the positive student teaching experience, did little to prepare me for the student apathy and a severe case of senioritis among my new students. The easy road of the first semester had suddenly gone into a sharp curve. I would be required to muster up all the determination I had in me to fight the daily attitude of just following a few simple guidelines and rules, passing economics, and graduating. The students were not interested in learning to fish. They preferred to have the fish given to them. A couple of terms come to mind when I recall the attitudes of the students. One term is disequilibrium, an economic term that I often related to students about unstable markets and their attitude about having to learn in a different way. Another term I learned in educational psychology is cognitive dissonance, which refers to causing an upheaval in the manner of doing things to which the mind had grown accustomed. Honestly, some of the students actually liked the changes, but so many were so resistant it made every day in class a struggle. Every day I had to answer questions about worksheets, notes, extra credit, and multiple other ways of earning non-academic credit. I managed by staying positive and constantly reassuring the students that the writing, group work, projects, and other non-traditional teaching methodologies would help make them more successful after high school. In the end, I think most were pleased that they had done well, and they were proud of the fact that they had survived Booth.

What they probably did not realize was that I had survived also. I must mention that once again there were people who believed in me and invested their time to visit my class and encourage me. Interestingly, one was the art teacher and the other was the Spanish teacher Lyn Slattery, both of whom were outside the box in their philosophies also. Ms. Cherones, ex-wife of the Executive Director of *Seinfeld*, was a perfect example of the typically artsy people who teach art. The new friends taught across the hall from each other and at the opposite end of the hall from me. They did visit my classroom on occasion, but most of the time I ventured down to their rooms to get encouragement. I also stopped by to watch them in class and was amazed at the attention and respect they got from their students. Their antics, teaching styles, and personalities demanded engagement from the students. The wonderful women constantly told me to focus on surviving the term and the students next year would be all mine. I hoped they would be correct.

Sink or Swim

At the end of the school year and during the summer, the most dramatic influence on my teaching would occur. The school had an Advanced Placement program in place with some very good courses and others that were not so good. The principal at the school went to great lengths to make sure that County High would provide any and all courses available at any other school. The system did not necessarily have the best facilities, but academics and course offerings emphasized the vision and direction of the school system. A trend to improve the buildings would occur later, unfortunately resulting in somewhat less emphasis on strong academic programs. The trade-off is very common in all school districts. Board members, superintendents, principals, and community developers love building programs. The opportunity to have his or her name placed on a plaque and attached to a building as a lasting memorial has great appeal to everyone in politics. There is less appeal to leaving a legacy of strong support of academic achievement.

The teacher who had the responsibility of the AP American Government and Economics program and I had become acquainted during my first semester. Perhaps he saw my youth and enthusiasm as necessary to help the program improve as well as an opportunity for him to step aside from the responsibility and accountability associated with AP and the very best students at the school. He was ready for another adventure and so was I.

Most students accept the notion that teachers are masters of the material they teach and regardless of the effectiveness of the methodologies seldom question the knowledge of the teacher. However, the most talented of our students are those that seriously question assertions made by a teacher unless there is substantial and convincing evidence that supports a new concept or way of thinking. A majority of the students in my AP classes were products of gifted programs in elementary and middle school. As a result, they were very experienced with the opportunity to think, solve problems, and to ask questions in order to verify what they were learning was in fact accurate and true. Many of the students also had parents who were professors at the University who possessed the more liberal concepts of teaching and learning. There would be no fooling of these students.

The teacher made note to me that he was entering another stage of his life and was looking at a possible administrative position for the last few years of his career in order to enhance his retirement. In Alabama, a person who retires from education draws a pension based on a percentage of the average of the three highest paid salaries within the last ten years of employment. Many teachers with administrative certification desire a stint at the close of their career in order to secure the highest possible retirement check. The practice is a very financially sound maneuver but sometimes results in less-than-effective school leadership.

The teacher was a master salesperson and attempted to lure me into the program by suggesting that the students who took the AP classes were highly motivated and gifted. All a person really needed to do was to provide the students with the textbook and tell them to read. I assume he thought I was looking for an easy job that would require less time and effort on my part. His reasoning and assumption about the class were proven to be completely incorrect based on the poor performance of the handful of students who bothered to take the College Board exam in order to earn college credit. I did not know very much about the program, but I was willing to learn. I was also willing to accept the challenge of providing instruction to students who were undoubtedly smarter than I was, but also knowing that regardless of their ability, the program would require a tremendous investment of time and energy on my part. We went to the principal together, and the result of the meeting was the opportunity for me to train for what would be one of the most rewarding experiences of my career and my life. The administration at the school arranged for me to attend two consecutive weeks in Advanced Placement workshops at the University of Alabama. It would be an exciting summer for a number of reasons.

Although my first experience as a teacher had not been all that I expected, I accepted what my teacher friends had told me that the next group of students would produce a much better attitude from the students. I was convinced more than ever that I was on a more effective track to my calling to teach. To be even more intensely involved in my career, I needed to move my family to the community where I was teaching. I had obviously made some positive impression on supervisors in the system. The school system knew my wife would need a job, and she was soon able to secure a teaching position. I would need to sell our house and buy another while I was busy preparing for the next year and attending the AP workshops. We soon found a house we liked and made a contingent offer based on the selling of the house where we lived. We had bought our current house in town following the house fire that had destroyed the one we had built out on the farm. The house was in foreclosure when we purchased it, and we were able to get it for a good price. Completing a few cosmetic improvements gave us the opportunity to sell the house and pocket some equity. However, as is always the case, the house did not sell as quickly as we hoped, and I made a decision to go ahead and purchase the new house and assume the old one would eventually sell. Despite the warnings from relatives, friends, and the banker, we would be making two house payments a month for a while. It was a leap of faith based on my belief that I was moving the way God wanted us to move. For three anxious months we waited, and then we finally got an offer for the home. In spite of the buyers nearly backing out of the deal at the last moment because of all the paperwork associated with home buying, we did close, and I experienced a great sense of relief.

My daughters were not exactly excited to be moving away from their friends. In fact, my oldest, who was now eleven, openly refused to go. She proclaimed that she would stay with grandparents and continue to go to school with her friends. After a great deal of counseling, reassuring, and promising, she finally gave in to the move. I always joke with her about it because after putting up such a fuss about moving, in two weeks at her new school it would have been more difficult to get her to move back than it was to get her to go along with the initial move. The girls' acceptance of the move made the change much easier for their mom and me.

The final stage of the move was leaving the church that had been so influential in my life and was now becoming just as important to my children. We visited around to a few churches and finally settled on one that was prominent in the community and was the church where many of my students attended. The music minister at the church was also the human resource director for the school system. Dr. Hinton had been very influential in helping me to get the job at County High. It seemed appropriate that we join the church. We had hoped the church would be most similar to the church we were leaving, but it soon occurred to us that it was not very similar. Southern Baptists take pride in the fact that each individual church has autonomy, and so each one is different on what is taught and the collective beliefs and interpretations of the members. The church was a great church, but we just did not feel like it was right for us. After a year, the pastor from our former church moved to a church close to the University campus, and we soon visited and moved our membership to Calvary Baptist, which would be our home for the next several years. At Calvary, our children became associated with a set of friends different from their school friends. Most of the students at the church attended the city or private schools. Our children became very active in their youth group and were associated with and led by some of the best adults in the church. I contend that the church's investment in my girls played the most significant part in their spiritual development. Just as their father's church had played such a pivotal part in his life, Calvary would provide the same guidance and training in theirs. Of all the developments and great things happening in my life, nothing was greater than to see my children learning and growing strong because of the caring investment made by the members of our church family.

However, the church was much more than a place that was good for my children. I aggressively agreed to an opportunity to teach a young adult Sunday school class that grew from four or five regular members to over forty in regular attendance. In the class, I was able to use my talent for teaching to serve the one who had given me the gift. The blessing I received from my study and preparation, along with the associations and relationships I developed with so many good people, helped me continue to grow in my spirituality. In fact, looking back now, I can argue that Calvary had as much impact on me as my home church. I will always be indebted to and thankful for Calvary Baptist Church for all they did for my children and me. Life was good and my children were wonderful, yet there was a longing and a lack of completeness that nagged at me. It would still be several years, but I would come face to face with situations and circumstances that would threaten all the great things that were happening in my life.

Reputation for Repudiation

Although I had been in the school for only the second semester of the previous year, I had managed to develop a reputation about the established standards in my classroom. Class schedules in schools are developed and set into place before school dismisses for the summer break. The first stage of the scheduling process is for students, with very limited counseling, to identify the classes they want to take the following year. The requests are the first stage in the development of a master schedule of the total number of classes taught for each subject in secondary schools or grade level in elementary school. Every school and every grade or subject have certain teachers that parents and students desire, as well as those they want to avoid. Other than the basic subjects of math, science, social studies, and English, students most often choose classes based on the accurate or inaccurate reputation of the teacher of the class. In my current position in charge of human resources, I often point out in meetings that the most important commodity in any school is the teacher. The success or failure of a particular "elective" class is mostly dependent on how popular the teacher is for the class. Recall that I stated earlier that teacher popularity is usually based on how easy or how demanding and productive the class is to the student. When students in secondary schools request a class and check the box for the particular class they desire, they often must have the teacher initial off on the request.

Based on the flow of students who came into my room prior to the end of school, I could tell that I had been a topic of discussion among the junior class who would be seniors the following year. Although there was no official announcement of my taking over the AP Government and Economics classes, all the students seemed to know I was the new teacher and things would be much different than the perception they had of the previous teacher. There was a great deal of uneasiness by many students about what they might be getting into by electing AP over the regular class. I used all my charm and assured each student that the class would be challenging but fair. I also encouraged students to take the class to better prepare themselves for college. When the master schedule came out, I had three classes of AP and two regular classes. When school started in the fall, twenty students had changed their schedules from AP to regular, but I maintained my three AP classes.

Amid all the changes in personal teaching responsibilities was a change in the room where I would teach. The former teacher did in fact acquire a job as an assistant principal at one of the feeder junior high schools, so I moved into his classroom that was in the newest wing at the school. The room was fabulous, and I had to do little cleaning to get it ready. I arranged the desks in my now-popular design with an aisle down the middle and my desk and storage at the back of the room. I would miss my friends in the other building, but the new room made up for the loss of support. I also knew immediately that the students now belonged to me, and I was excited to get started. There was a great deal of excitement from me and the students in the air. The students had heard about my dissident ideas and repudiation of traditional learning, and there was a great deal of curiosity to find out about all the fuss. It was exciting to confirm my expectations I had for myself, as well as the expectations from my colleagues and those who had encouraged and invested in me to this point. My constructive fear of failure would motivate me to work harder than I had worked for A&P, on the farm, or in school. My vision and focus would be totally on developing effective instruction and motivating students so they could see clearly their personal mission in life as well as I saw my own.

FOUR

During my twenty-five plus years in education, I have participated in countless discussions and debates with colleagues and college personnel concerning the question of teaching as an art or a science. I have already expressed my opinion and concluded that achieving greatness in any profession requires passion, determination, and hard work. I am also a believer that all people have talents and gifts. As a result of my exposure to music in high school, along with the influence of probably the most gifted educator with whom I have ever been associated, I have developed a love and appreciation for many forms of music, including bluegrass, country, rock and roll, and classical. My colleagues exhibit a certain degree of confusion by my favorite song lists on my computer in my office that includes classic rock, as well as *Phantom of the Opera* and *Les Miserables*. Although I am a major fan and appreciate music for many reasons, I am not by any stretch of the imagination a gifted musician. I do play

104

a little guitar and can carry a tune with a large enough bucket, but my enjoyment of music is exponentially greater than any gift I have. Had I spent more time practicing trumpet and guitar, I could have been much better than I am, but no amount of training would ever make me great; therefore, I conclude that in order for me to be a true musician, I must have a gift for music. I also believe in order to be a teacher, individuals who pursue the career must possess an art for teaching that must be cultivated and enriched with training and experience. The science of teaching without the art or gift, at the very best, will develop only a marginally successful teacher. On the other hand, a gift for teaching without training and experience will equate to a similar level of proficiency. The most dynamic and successful teachers possess an art for teaching and develop and nurture the science.

I recently went shopping with my wife, which means I spent my time sitting and watching people. On this occasion, there were two saxophone musicians performing in separate common areas of the shopping area. One of the performers was a veteran musician who has spent his life learning, performing, and teaching music. I was amazed to listen to and witness his obvious talent. Even more impressive was the other saxophonist who was a teenager.

Without taking into consideration his age and experience, it was obvious to me that his talent and ability was at least equal to and probably greater than the veteran player. What I experienced from both musicians was a very special gift. If I had played saxophone since childhood and practiced every day, I could not achieve the level of talent each performer demonstrated. There are many very good musicians in the world, but there are very few that are great. Professional musicians who make a living in music must possess a musical gift at some exceptional level or they would not professionally survive. Unfortunately-- and this is a statement that will offend many in my profession-- there are too many educators who have neither a gift nor talent to teach. In addition, there is a misguided notion perpetuated by colleges of education, as well as state and local school systems, that we can provide professional development and other training and make anyone a teacher. Preparation can make people better, but it will fail to yield the required proficiency necessary to be a great teacher. Regardless of the investment in training and preparation, I could never be able to perform on the saxophone the way the two people did at the shopping center. In education, few barriers exist that prevent individuals without talent from becoming teachers, and unfortunately, many should not be in the profession.

I am not saying that every teacher can or should be masters of their profession. No profession can truthfully boast that every individual in a particular field is the very best. However, in almost every profession in the free market system, a level of proficient and productive individual performance identifies and replaces untalented or incompetent employees with individuals who can perform better. Many have argued that tenure and teacher unions have created a system that tolerates and protects teachers who do not perform their duties with an acceptable level of proficiency. However, I think the problem is perhaps more basic. Schools boards, administrators, and influential members of the school community often produce a political climate that serves individual interests and fails to provide for the recruitment and hiring of the best-qualified and most gifted candidates for positions. Although nepotism and cronyism are not publicly accepted and are even illegal, the practice is at the very least a substantial factor in hiring teachers and administrators. Once hired and receiving tenure, teacher unions and tenure laws protect the individual, but those factors have nothing to do with initial hiring. The same professional standards in private business and industry do not exist in education. However, the social and political climate in public education will not support the financial compensation required to attract the very best as long as there are obvious examples of incompetency in the profession. The situation creates a continuous loop in which policy makers and citizens will not honor the profession and compensate accordingly until the elimination or reduction of incompetency. The lack of accountability and benefits will continue to attract many who do not possess the art to teach nor the desire to improve in the science of teaching. The failure to attract and retain the highest quality individuals as teachers and to deal effectively with malpractice results in a system of mediocrity. Mediocrity can produce only mediocre results.

Why Do Doctors *Practice* Medicine?

In every position I have held in education, there was always the misperception on my part to believe that the transition for me would be easy and that I knew all I needed to know about the position. This was never more evident than my first full year as a teacher. Although I had struggled the spring semester the previous year, I concluded that my major obstacle was dealing with students who were unhappy with the dramatic change in their school world. My mentors were correct in the fact that my first full year the students would be more accepting of me, resulting in teaching and learning being more fun. I am confident that I have a passion for teaching and that I possess some level of giftedness as a teacher, but I soon learned that I did not have all the answers. I realized that simply because I felt my teaching was a calling did not make me anything special. A tremendous amount of work was necessary to utilize any gift I had. In effect, I discovered why doctors, lawyers, dentists, and other professionals begin to *practice* their trade after they finish training. For the first couple of years in the classroom, I would be practicing being a teacher. In fact, the practicing never stops. Good and great teachers are constantly experimenting with ideas and reflecting on results based on informal formative assessments by asking questions or even looking into the faces of students to determine if they really understand and master a concept or idea.

I firmly believed then as I do now that I do have a gift to be able to communicate ideas, motivate learners, assess learning, as well as clarifying when my point is not getting across and re-teaching. The art of teaching also means the ability to be patient with others and accept the fact that not every student is as passionate about learning as some others are. Moreover, I have discovered there are very few who are as enthusiastic as I am. However, a big part of the art of teaching is the ability to develop and foster passion in others. Just as important is the ability to utilize the science of teaching by experimenting with strategies and methodologies, abandoning what fails, and refining things that work. Good science, accompanied by art, improves teaching and learning.

A majority of what I know and profess now about teaching and learning is a result of the seven years I was in the classroom. As I look back, it seems like a vast experiment. Without a doubt, the AP training cleared my head and helped me design a pattern that would prove to be successful in the advanced classes and in my regular classes. However, my instincts about students and learning played a more significant role in every activity I designed and implemented in the classroom. The goals I developed for what I wanted students to know and to be able to do when they left my class were rooted in my gift, the passion for which I felt obligated to assure that students obtained goals, additional training, and the hard work and determination fostered by my array of experiences outside of education. Misinterpreted, my passion about my career may seem arrogant to critics. There may be some truth in that I believe my gift allows me to understand what others may not see or appreciate about the magnitude of the responsibility we have as educators. I refer to this as "getting it," and in my career I have worked with many teachers and educators who "got it." Unfortunately, the numbers of people in the field who do not get it far outnumber those who do.

I consider my greatest gift as an educator to be the ability to see the big picture and to observe, analyze, predict, and take action to improve my role in education. The source of my greatest frustration, and probably my biggest weakness, is working with people who are unable to see, hear, and react to what I see as barriers to effective teaching and learning. Interestingly, I often witnessed that same personal frustration in my classroom with my students. However, I felt my role was to enlighten my students and to provoke them into appreciating and understanding the purpose for learning. I also desired for the students to value the skills they developed and the subsequent impact of learning on their future. I took on the role in the classroom as a trailblazer to lead my students through a jungle of information to use in developing answers and solutions to personal, political, and social problems they would encounter in life. That role has not changed in any of the positions I have held over the years. Every day in the classroom was practice for the next day. Every year was a prelude for the following year. Every position would be experience for the next, and every experience was an investment for the future.

Glory Days

> "Glory days, well, they'll pass you by,
> Glory days in the wink of a young girl's eye,
> Glory days, glory days."
>
> *Bruce Springsteen*

I consider my seven years in the classroom my glory days and they did pass me by quickly. However, there is seldom a day that that I do not reflect on a particular lesson, student, or incident that happened in the classroom that provided a fond and eternal memory. During my teaching years, I also completed my master's program in secondary education and then an additional add-on certification in administration in the summer of 1996. In every college class, I always looked for ways to apply what I was learning to my classroom. Seeking additional degrees by being in school always made me a better teacher and administrator by keeping me up to date on issues and for sparking ideas for my practice. A particular example was student surveys.

During my last year at the University, I had taken a political science class in research survey methods. Although I did not enjoy a particular project in the class, which involved actually conducting a statewide telephone survey one evening, the class did provide me with the knowledge of how to construct and conduct surveys that would be accurate - within a 3% to 5% margin of error. Almost immediately, I saw where the knowledge would be useful in a high school government class, and during my teaching years, my classes annually conducted student surveys. I shared with the students what I had learned about effective and proper sequence of questioning in order to get an acceptable margin of error from the responses. Most interesting, the political surveys were not only accurate for determining what the students were thinking, they turned out to be an accurate measure for what their parents thought. Even though teens try to rebel and be different in thought and actions from their parents, most inevitably do follow in the ideology and opinions of the parents. Where else would children develop views and opinions about politics than from overhearing their parents talk? This phenomenon may be changing in today's culture because of technology and a child having much more exposure to other voices, but the family is still the most socializing factor for children in both good and bad ways.

After initially notifying the media of the survey projects, the local paper and television stations became expectant of the student surveys prior to elections, and the results were a reflection of how parents felt and about how they would vote on issues and candidates. The media, in order to help predict what the results would actually be in elections, began to call the school and me and ask about the surveys. The increase in attention from the media made my students much more engaged and motivated, and with my assistance, developed good surveys with very accurate conclusions. Keep in mind that the surveys and other projects did not interfere with or replace the student's active engagement covering the course of study. They also involved cross-curricular activities such as writing questions that were grammatically correct, counting and totaling responses, calculating percentages, and writing summaries of the findings. The activities did not replace but supplemented the curriculum. Never did any projects in my classroom replace the standards or objectives for the course. They did, however, reinforce and add relevance to the study. My goal was to make government and economics come to life in the classroom by helping students realize the impact and importance of understanding and participating in our political and economic systems. By developing and administering student surveys and providing the results to the media, the students were already actively participating in a common practice in American politics.

It has always amused me when many people, including my mother, are upset with something happening in government or the economy. The president is most often the target of the frustration and criticism. Whether it was destiny, luck, insight from the founding fathers, or divine intervention, the United States has succeeded in large part because of the checks and balances associated with the division of powers of the federal government. Presidents have the responsibilities to sign or veto bills and faithfully execute the laws passed by both houses of Congress. Presidents do not make laws. In the event of a law's unconstitutionality, the Supreme Court uses the power of judicial review to overturn laws that violate the Constitution. Many students had seen School-House Rock's "I'm Just a Bill," so the bill passing simulation activity that I devised was not very alien to them. However, the students would have to adjust to the politics involved in creating legislation and making laws.

I divided the class into a House of Representative, Senate, and executive branch with a president and vice president. Each student had to write a bill that he or she would introduce in his or her assigned member house. The president would also write a bill to submit to Congress through a member he or she enlisted to present the bill. The key to success was getting the bill presented, voted on, and passed. Students had to present the bill and lobby for passage in the other legislative house. In order to become law, the bill required a signature by the president. The president could also veto the bill, which killed the bill or sent it back to the legislature for amendment. To add a consequence to the activity and provide for assessment, each student's grade was determined by how far the bill progressed in the process. If a bill failed to pass either house or was vetoed by the president, the student would amend and resubmit the bill for reconsideration. The final judgment on the merit and constitutionality of the bill belonged to one of my AP classes, which acted as the Supreme Court. It is not difficult to imagine the chaos involved as students were using multiple tactics in order to get a bill through Congress and signed by the president. While it may not have appeared orderly and organized, the activity proved to be a very effective learning experience for all, including the AP class that had to determine the constitutionality of the bill.

On one particular day and during the middle of the chaos, the assistant principal came into my room to deliver a school memo. He did not say anything on his visit, but I could tell by the look on his face that he was confused. He did not question me at the time, but a few minutes after he left the room he opened the door and walked toward me at the back of the room. He said he was curious and just had to ask what was going on with all the noise and activity. I called the class to order and asked one of the students to tell him what we were doing. After the student finished a summary of the activity, the assistant principal simply said, "Great job, please continue," and left the room. I could not have been more satisfied and proud. From time to time during the remaining school year, students would ask to do the activity again. Learning can and should be engaging and fun!

I continued to use the media to motivate students and to keep the community informed about the great things that were happening in the classroom. I did not know it at the time, but I had obtained the nickname *Hollywood* among the faculty at the school. Over the course of my career, I have often heard educators and others criticize the media for taking comments out of content and misquoting statements in broadcasts and publications. On the contrary, I have always been delighted with reporting and never had an issue with reporting the message I wanted to get out in the reports. I made friends in the media, and I was on a first name basis with most of the local media personalities.

The media seemed to be the most interested in stories related to politics. We once staged a mock debate between candidates for governor with two students assuming the roles of the candidates. The staging for the event was in the gym with backdrops and lighting that would have been appropriate for a real debate. One of the actual candidates happened to be in the area when the debate was to occur, and the media told him about the students at my school and the debate. He sent a message to the school stating that he wished he could attend, but scheduling prevented him from coming. He did send his personal regards with a media representative and wished *her* the best. The debate was remarkable, and the two candidates made me very proud with their performance. Under the glare of lights, several hundred students, a newspaper reporter, and three television news stations, each student and a team of aides and supporters performed well enough that the exercise accurately resembled an actual political campaign – including the look, sound, and rhetoric. The story got amazing media coverage, and the students talked about it for weeks.

The current emphasis on classroom instruction focuses on *student-centered instruction*. The concept involves the teacher acting as a facilitator of learning and abandoning the traditional concept where the teacher is standing and lecturing at the front of the room and giving assignments. Students sit in rows of desks, take notes, and learn by listening to the teacher. In a student-centered environment, the students take an active role in their learning with investigation and discovery taking place independently or in a small group. The teacher's responsibilities are primarily in the planning and establishing the structure for the students to work. Although a great deal of my instruction centered on lecture and discussion, the students often were engaged in small group work. The big activities such as the debate provided the students with the opportunity to use creativity and individual talents to learn in a student-centered environment. I was always amazed at what students could do when I allowed them the opportunity and provided a little structure and motivation to their efforts. The students never let me down. I was in effect investing my time and energy in helping students learn to think and act as independent and active learners. It was my hope that I was preparing them for a productive life.

There was always a major project or activity in progress in my classrooms. I continued to utilize my writing project from my internship with great success, but the students also participated in a multitude of other projects. I would often begin class stating that I had a brainstorm the evening before or in the shower, and the students would respond with something along the lines of, "What has he come up with now?" Sometimes we would plan together on exactly where the project would lead, and sometimes I had it all laid out for them. In any event, the students were always anticipating that something out of the ordinary was about to happen. Differentiated instruction, as well as major projects and writing, along with daily lessons that included active discussions, group work, and other "outside the box" things I could come up with to keep the students engaged characterized the atmosphere of our classroom. I was at the top of my game and personally motivated by the student performance and learning that was happening before my eyes.

I Will. You Will. We Will.

The key to a successful learning environment is the result of a relationship or partnership that develops between the teacher and the students. The relationship for me consists of three factors: what the teacher does, what the students do, and what the teacher and the students do together. Teachers are very good at laying out expectations for students that usually relate to behavior, organization, responsibility, and performance. The expectations are usually in the form of written class rules or a syllabus that outlines precise expectations from the students. Discussions take place with the class at the beginning of the school year and are reiterated as needed during the school year to focus on violations or deviations from the teacher's expectations. The consequences of non-compliance for the students and the teacher's response too often constitute the role of the teacher. In the worst cases, the relationship becomes very similar to the example of incarcerated individuals and a prison guard. In the old days, the similarity between schools and prisons was much more similar than different. During one of my college degree programs, the class actually visited a state prison to observe and consider the similarities. I am all in on standards and expectations for students, but in order for a healthy and productive class to function, there is a much more complex arrangement that must exist.

I have mentioned several times the number of investments made in me by those who believed and must have seen something in me that I did not see in myself. Teachers should see all students as open receptacles for knowledge and understanding and recognize that every student has a special talent or gift. More importantly, teachers should help students see talents and gifts within themselves. It is easy to tell students that they are special and they have a purpose, but more importantly, continuous examples of commitment from educators demonstrate to each student an understanding of the relationship between commitment and achievement. The most apparent and effective demonstration of any teacher's commitment to students can be realized when the students see the results of the teacher's work and preparation directed at student learning. Teachers provide evidence of commitment to students with detailed assignments through grading rubrics, explicit directions for classroom and other activities, returning graded assignments in a timely manner, celebrating with students when they succeed and encouraging them when they fail, and constantly exhibiting excitement and enthusiasm for the career they have chosen.

It is extremely difficult and maybe impossible to fool students when they see the teacher every day and witness a lack of planning and excitement about the day's activity. Many times I have overheard students discussing among themselves the work ethic of teachers. They recognized and responded to teachers they knew were doing the job well. I did not ever want to be the subject of students in another classroom discussing how the government teacher was unprepared for or apathetic toward student learning. I tried always to demonstrate a strong work ethic and to remind students that I was willing to work very hard at my job. I announced often that in return I expected the same hard work from each of them.

I also announced to students that the numerous exciting things happening in the classroom were all reflections of what *we* were doing together. The students would not be able to participate in an exciting class where active learning was taking place every day if I did not work diligently to provide learning opportunities that engaged students and produced student-centered learning. On the other hand, if the students did not respond with the same enthusiasm and determination, my efforts would be fruitless. It took all of us working together to make learning productive and fun. In promoting and developing an "*I, you,* and *we"* relationship, the classroom becomes a place where both the students and the teacher are excited about each day and every opportunity to witness real learning. I made it a point for us to celebrate together when great things happened. When a "failure to learn" happened, I accepted my part in the failure and helped students see how and where we could have done better.

Although Advanced Placement student personalities were different, the curriculum was far more in depth, and the pace was at light speed, my AP classes were founded on the same *I, you*, and *we* relationship. The scope of the AP program requirements is so vast that student initiative, determination, and independence is even more imperative than that of regular classes. The mastery of the material and the maturity level of the students required to successfully complete the course and then make a passing score on the College Board exam are far beyond any introductory college class at any university. Since passing the College Board exam allows a student to earn college credit and to be exempt from taking the class in college, the College Board makes sure that students have mastered the material. Colleges and universities demand high proficiency since a student's passing the exam eliminates the student paying tuition for a class for which credit is earned in high school. The teacher resources that accompany the college textbook, including test banks, are also difficult to obtain from book publishers since universities pressure the publishers against the dispersion of the materials. The result is that there are no shortcuts for students pursuing college credit in the AP program. Therefore, the teacher and the students must be of one accord in the study. The three relational factors of *I, we, and you* are even more important for the program to be successful.

I worked very hard to develop and nurture a mutual relationship of trust and respect with my gifted AP students who often saw things differently than I did. It was a personal challenge for me to be prepared to respond to students who were incredibly intelligent and highly motivated to succeed. Often their questions and insights were beyond what I had anticipated, but I never indicated to them that I knew everything. Many times, I had to confess my inability to answer their question, but in what would become a very effective teaching practice, we would explore the possible solutions together and most often arrive at a consensus response. I have to confess that I learned as much from the students as they learned from me. I held them in the highest regard, and I believe they felt the same about me.

A couple of revelations occurred in my first AP Macroeconomics class that would solidify my standing with the students. Since the group would be my first to take the College Board exam, I was extremely anxious and very worried that I would overlook an important concept the students would encounter on the exam. The exam consists of fifty multiple-choice questions of the highest caliber, and I made sure the students would become accustomed to that level of thinking by preparing my summative tests at as close to the same level as I could. As one would expect, the students had serious concerns about my tests. They believed I was splitting hairs or trying to trick them with the answers. Students addressing concerns every time we went back over the exam became common, and I spent substantial time preparing to explain answers. I dealt with the anxiety and skepticism of the students by reminding them that I was only trying to get them ready for the level of questions they would see on the College Board exam.

Another part of the exam is the free response to an economic situation in which the students would have to respond with a narrative and graphs and charts based on their analysis and proposed solution to the economic problem. Again, we had practiced the procedure many times in class, and I always reminded the students of the attempt to mimic what they would see in the future. On one occasion, after my review of free response stems from previous exams, it came to me that a relatively new economic concept phenomenon of stagflation had not appeared on any previous exams. Almost as a gift of enlightenment for me, I predicted that the concept would be a perfect situation for the scholars to address on the exam. We worked through a solution for stagflation, defined as the economic condition where there is very high unemployment, and inflation is occurring at the same time in the economy. The condition had actually existed in the United States in the early 1980s. President Reagan and Federal Reserve Chairman Paul Volker had the national responsibility and authority to take steps to correct the economic instability. In class we created a response based on what the President and the Federal Reserve did with interest rates that painfully resolved the problem. I repeatedly warned the students to be ready because I was predicting that the free response question would be to address stagflation. The proclamation was a major risk. However, someone has said that without risk there can be no reward, and good leaders are always risk takers.

As the time for the College Board exam approached, I became more anxious in anticipation. The results on the exam would be an indicator for the school administration and me of the actual quality of instruction and learning the students were receiving in my classroom. I was confident that I had done all I knew to do, but I had not convinced myself that I had done all that I had needed to do. My stress level far exceeded the students, who were confident and relaxed. I just prayed that my efforts would be justified by the scores at least not being an embarrassment to me or the students. The time for accountability had come. The College Board exam was the measure of my competency just as end-of-the-year assessments should be for teachers today.

The school counselor administered the exam at the Church of God down the street from the school. Following the exam, most of the students came running to my room. Never have I witnessed students more excited about a test. The students inaccurately proclaimed me a genius for predicting the exact free response question presented on the test. I had actually gotten very lucky. They also assured me that they were not intimidated by the multiple-choice section of the exam - not so much luck but practice and preparation. All the students said they felt really good about how they had done. Later, the very few students who had chosen not to take the exam would lament to the others that it was a mistake not to take the exam. I felt great and extremely fortunate, but I knew that the real accountability would come in July when the scores came to the school. I would have to sweat it out for a month. In the meantime, the process of getting new students to sign up for the following year was the next objective. I felt that the students and I had done our best, and by continuing the "I, you, and we" relationship, we would now start the process of recruitment for next year's group of AP students.

Catching a Big Fish

Excluding all the personal happiness in my life from my childhood memories of grandparents and parents, my spiritual experiences and encouragement from a wonderful church family, and the birth of two perfect daughters, I had experienced very few career experiences that convinced me that there was a special purpose for my life until I began my career in education. Obviously, I had learned tremendous lessons from the experience at the A&P, the automotive factory, and the farm. However, each of the career paths had failed to provide me with any assurance that I was in any way on a mission to fulfill my destiny. I am certain I am not unique in believing I have a special purpose in life, but I do know that the passion for personal achievement is and has always been substantial in my life. The combination of my innate passion, along with the desire to succeed based on the investment of others and myself, I have believed since late childhood that my destiny was to make some mark on the world. None of my previous career paths had satisfied any longing to contribute meaningfully or to make any improvement to the world. In education, I had found the way that I was to have meaning in my life. My purpose was to teach and promote learning in young people and to improve the profession for which talent, experience, and investment had prepared and destined me. The notion of education being my purpose would need to be confirmed when the AP scores arrived in July.

I have described my principal, Mr. Walker, to some degree previously. I do need to add that he was a man of few words and mostly all business. As I did mention earlier, his personality was similar to what I perceived the personality of Paul "Bear" Bryant, who was known as being a traditional, direct, and no-nonsense football coach at Alabama. Since I was a nine-month employee at the time and not at school in July, I got a phone call from the school, and Mr. Walker's growling voice asked me to come to the school. My AP scores had arrived. He did not say a word more and gave no indication in his voice or mannerisms to indicate there was or was not a problem with the results. I was extremely nervous and excited at the same time as I raced to the school. The principal and his two assistants were in the main office when I arrived. I reminded him I was there about the AP scores, and he dryly stated he was a little shocked but hoped I would not be too disappointed. We entered his office with the assistants coming in behind, and I sat in a chair in front of his desk as he reached into his desk and pulled out an envelope. I knew that the scores would range from 1 to 5 with a 3 considered eligible for college credit, a 4 being excellent, and a 5 indicating complete mastery. He called the names of a couple of students who had scored a 2 and did not meet the cut score. I knew the names were of students who were not the best students in the class, but I did not have time to react until he announced that ten students had scored a 3, five had scored a 4, and three had scored a 5. I was still in shock and unable to react when a grin came across Mr. Walker's face as he told me I had done a great job. In my most humble and true educator fashion, I told him that the results were not because of me but the wonderful students. He looked at me, continuing to grin, and simply said, "Right."

I was beyond excited and spent most of the afternoon calling the students and congratulating them for the accomplishment. It was one of the most rewarding days of my teaching career. Over the course of the next six years, my students would continue to thrill me with their results on the test. Almost without waver, 85% of my students took the government and the economics exams each year, and 85% of those that took the exam scored a 3 or above. I was always disappointed for the students who did not pass, but the thrill for those who unexpectedly passed made up for any disappointment I experienced. It is interesting that the student I remember the most was not one at the top of the senior class or who had an exceptional ACT score, but one who did possess confidence and determination. I suspect that her athletic experience had taught her the positive effects of hard work and commitment.

Christy was a cheerleader who had come to me during recruiting asking about the program and trying to make up her mind if she could handle the rigor of the class. She did possess the wisdom to realize that the class, even if she did not score high enough to gain college credit, would benefit her in college. She worked as hard as any student I had ever taught and was always pleasant and cooperative, a bit apprehensive, but full of confidence and determination to hold her own with the rest of the class. She managed to sneak out a *B* in class, but fell just short on the College Board exam. I often use her when people tell me that the AP program is not for average students. In my opinion, an average student can do well in any AP class if they work hard and maintain a positive and determined attitude. Christy is one of the students I remember most.

Unfortunately, the other students for whom I have the most vivid memories were the students in AP and regular classes with exceptional ability, but they treated the class with the same apathy and unambitious attitude that had done little to affect the outcome in most other classes and had produced little more than a passing grade. There are many of this type of students in schools. In fact, many of the students who drop out of school are some of the most talented. Often, a student being bored and above the learning level of other students is the explanation for the phenomenon. I will agree that there are cases in which boredom may be a cause, but I feel most likely that capable but poor-performing students do not have the ambition and grit to work hard for personal achievement. Perhaps the student was not encouraged by parents, lacked personal motivation, or maybe had been able to make good grades without much effort. For whatever reason, underachieving students have always presented me with the most problems and broke my heart as an educator. As I have mentioned, one of my major responsibilities as an educator is to invest in students and to help them see they are capable of achieving so much. That responsibility followed me from the classroom into the school and district offices.

Many educators and policy makers today feel we must go to students and address their social and emotional needs if we are to help them perform well and be actively engaged in learning. My philosophy has always been to demonstrate with my words and actions that no matter their personal situation, learning would provide them with an avenue to overcome most of the issues facing them. I use my own story to illustrate what education can do for a student who may not live in a nice neighborhood, wear stylish clothes, or possess many things most think are necessary to succeed. My tool for helping young people is to teach them to learn and to love learning. I can get assistance when there is a genuine need, but my mission is to provide a mechanism for improving their life by investing my talent in helping students become successful and productive. I consider what I do as an opportunity to give students the knowledge and skills that will benefit them for the rest of their life. If I can only help students get through a tough issue during the present and not prepare them for the future, then I have failed them as an educator. If I manage what I do as an educator correctly, I will take care of the present and the future at the same time.

FIVE

Scott was a student who came to my classroom with a tremendous amount of baggage. He was widely known as being difficult to manage in the classroom and lived a fast-paced life in the evenings and on the weekends. Teachers in the lower grades had warned me about Scott. He had a very volatile temper and showed little restraint in expressing his personal views or his disagreement with other students, teachers, and even administrators. He had a reputation as a bad dude, and so when the new principal, a former assistant, encouraged us to pick a student to mentor for the school year, I naturally selected Scott. Other teachers thought I had completely lost my mind based on the experiences each previously had with Scott in class. It would be a challenge, but I was determined to make Scott my project.

When Scott came into my class for the first time, I could hardly believe my eyes. He was as good-looking as any

136

guy at the school. His clothes looked good, and he was athletic enough that he probably could have excelled in any sport. However, he chose not to play sports I am sure because he could not get along well with coaches. I did my usual introductions during that class, talked about my philosophy, and explained why learning would be fun and beneficial. An explanation about how we would be working and learning together included the expectations I had for both students and myself. I made a special effort to look eye to eye with Scott. Based on my warnings from other teachers about Scott, I assume that most of them had avoided any sort of contact with him as an "out of sight and out of mind" mentality. It is best not to poke a sleeping lion.

At first, Scott's body language indicated to me an attitude of skepticism and perhaps defiance. However, as I continued to explain how the class would operate and that the class would be different from any other class they had experienced, his expression changed, and I saw that I had his attention. I have always attempted to use humor in instruction, and so I used all my personal experience and resources to try to engage Scott and the rest of the class. By the end of the first class, his expression had changed from the typical troubled student scowl, subtle remarks, and negative demeanor to a look that seemed to me as curiosity and a little confusion. Perhaps his greatest confusion showed when I walked by his desk, bent over, and asked if he would stay a few minutes after class.

As Scott approached me standing at the front of the room after class, a small grin on his face indicated to me that he may have been thinking he was about to get the usual warnings about his behavior and the dire circumstances that would occur when there was a problem. I stuck out my hand for a handshake and told him I just wanted him to know that I was happy to have him in the class. I did notice his hand was a little clammy, evidence of a little nervousness. It further indicated to me that he was not as bad as others thought he was. I told him of the initiative for each teacher at the school to pick one student to mentor during the year, and that I had chosen him. The grin widened, and it appeared he was a little embarrassed. I continued and told him that I had heard all the things and been warned that he would be difficult, but I had discounted everything I had heard. He would be starting over in my class, and I expected more from him than compliance. I expected him to take an active role in class activities and use his obvious influence with other students to make sure everyone else participated in class. In effect, I wanted him to be a leader in the class, and I fully expected him to do his job well. He never disappointed me.

As it turned out, there were other strong leaders in the class, and most notable was Amber. Amber possessed the same strong will as Scott, and there developed a healthy competition between the two that worked to the advantage of my instruction and the learning of the others in the class. Although the two were very much alike, they often had opposing views on issues that resulted in heated. I made sure in all group activities that they were never in the same group. Both students took command of the class when discussions and debates occurred, and each placed specific demands and expectations on other students in their group during activities, when inevitably each assumed the primary leadership role. If discussions or debates got a little out of hand or grumbling about assignments erupted, Amber and Scott could bring the class to order as quickly as I could. It was amazing. It was like having teaching assistants in the class. I often used a trick of initiating a discussion about a particular topic and then stopping and announcing that the concepts were probably more appropriate for my AP classes. Scott and Amber would have none of that. In their minds they were every bit as capable as any student, and they were surely not going to allow the geeks in AP to learn more than they would.

My room was at the far end of the school complex, connecting the old and new buildings with a long glass hall that had no rooms and often no supervision. As one would expect, there was often trouble in the area. On one occasion, the intercom came on in my room during class change right before Scott's class period was to begin. Most of my students were already in the room as I stood at the door. Suddenly, the office announced for me to get to the glass hall to take care of a fight. I rushed from my room and sprinted out the door and up the corridor to the glass hall. When I arrived, the fight was over, and another teacher was escorting the perpetrators to the office. I assumed the role of clearing the hall and moving anxious and rowdy students on to class. As I turned to make my way back to my room, I literally ran face to face with Scott who had followed me to the glass hall. In my excitement of the moment, I yelled and asked him what he was doing there. His response was one I will never forget. In a calm and reassuring voice, Scott stated that he knew the situation could be bad and that he was there to cover my back. The student with attitude and behavior issues that teachers had warned me about was willing and able to do whatever he could to be by my side just in case things got nasty. I knew without any doubt that the relationship encouraged by the principal and the decision I had made to select Scott as the student I would select had worked beyond my wildest expectations. I believe Scott would have taken a bullet for me. On the way back to the room, I tried to explain to him that maybe it was not in his best interest to have followed me, but warning him did no good. The loyalty that had developed was so strong that had another incident happened when we got back to the room, he would have been behind me watching my back again.

What had turned Scott around and made him a model student in my class? It did not happen because I tried to win his confidence by counseling or preaching to him on being a better student or person. Most definitely, it did not happen by my taking a common authoritative position and instituting punitive measures to address his issues. He was not scared of me - it is hard to imagine him fearing anything or anybody. I think his turnaround was the result of respect earned by honestly communicating my mission and vision for the class, recognizing and encouraging his personal qualities in a positive manner, utilizing his leadership by placing trust in him, and reinforcing his good behavior with recognition. Most of all, I think the investment I made in him and the class with my hard work and planning that was always done in the hope of engaging the students on a daily basis, earned his and their respect. My position as teacher in the class gave me legal authority, but my efforts to work for students in order to prepare them for the future gave me legitimate authority. I think Scott worked hard and was conscientious because I had worked so hard to model the behavior I expected from students. For whatever reason, the connection and the relationship I made with Scott on the principles of "I, you, and we" encouraged him and most students to perform well as a way of saying "thank you" for my commitment to them.

I ran into Scott a few years after high school at a home improvement store where he was working in the home and garden department. He was doing very well with the store and had developed an intense interest in flowers, plants, and other aspects of landscaping. He also said that he was planning on going to college and getting a degree in horticulture. We also discussed high school, and he talked about how important my class was for him. He also mentioned that he had not actually graduated from high school because he had failed senior English with a 59 - one point short of a passing grade. He admitted that he had not worked well in the class and that he and the teacher did not get along very well. In all honesty, I have a hard time accepting the fact that the teacher could prevent him from graduating over one point when so much of a score in a classroom is considerably subjective. Knowing the English teacher, I think that it is probable that she was making one final statement about her authority and power in Scott's life. I am sure they fought a long battle during the year, and she felt she had won. How could Scott have done so well in my class and failed by one point in English? It was not his inability to think and reason. It was not because he could not write because he had written many papers for me that were very good. The teacher and Scott, without any doubt, had not established a mutual *I, you,* and *we* relationship. The "we" was missing.

After a few more years, I ran into Scott again, and he did get a degree and was successful and happy. I hope and pray that I was able in some way to provide some of the investment into his future. If so, and I think I did make a wise investment, the dividends for Scott, his family, society, and me are well worth the effort from everyone involved in his life. Amber became a very talented and highly regarded teacher and now works for a company teaching preparation classes for the ACT exam. Scott's and her success, along the success of so many other students, provide me with a tremendous amount of fulfillment and satisfaction in the career I have chosen.

Outside the Box - Within the Circle

Many educators and other professionals speak of being "outside the box" as an admirable quality that is encouraged by managers and supervisors. In reality, most people in any organization who advocate and practice a change in conventional thinking and methods are often considered disruptive to what is normal and the correct way of doing things. It is usually after success from creative thinking that breaks with the norm when recognition for being a rebel becomes an endearing characteristic. Steve Jobs and Apple Computer is an obvious example. Jobs and two partners set up a shop in a garage and began to develop a personal computer that has grown to a company that could buy a small country. Microsoft, Facebook, and Twitter all developed from quirky ideas by people some would consider a little strange. A woman named Kim Levine created a microwavable pillow with soothing heat using her sewing machine, some cloth, and raw corn. The result of her simple idea has been millions of dollars in profit from sales on Amazon (a unique idea also) and at Saks Fifth Avenue.

It seems as if the key to success in any area involves thinking outside the box and taking risks. The most successful educational programs today are those associated

144

with new ideas about teaching and learning. Whenever a school or school system improves learning, other schools want to know the secrets, and everyone "jumps on the bandwagon" and engages in the same or similar activities. Once everyone knows about a new and exciting idea, the idea is no longer new and the novelty, along with the effectiveness, eventually subsides. Starting a new computer company in my garage today would most likely result in failure. Just because it worked for Steve Jobs does not mean it will work for me. It is the novelty of an idea and the entrepreneurship of the individual or individuals that produces the exciting and the most remarkable results.

I prefer to think of my teaching years more as "thinking outside the box and within a circle." I felt that every day I had to think of something new and exciting in order to engage students. I wish I could say that every day in my class involved something new, but that would require little sleep and no life outside of teaching. However, new ideas were common enough in my classes that students often walked up to me at the door and asked a simple question that was a wonderful compliment and a great motivation for me to surprise them as often as possible. The simple question was, "Mr. Booth, what are we doing today?" The question did not imply a hope that I would say "nothing" because they knew better than that. I was compelled to think outside the box, but I had to keep in mind the circle of relevance for the activity and the concepts the students were to master. The inquiry about each day's activity told me the students were eager to see if we were doing something exciting and engaging. I always accepted the question as flattery and loved to say that they needed to put on thinking caps because they would need them. When I told them I had a brainstorm about some activity or project, they became cautious and excited at the same time. They knew the activity would be interesting, but it would also require a good deal of work from them - the "you" part of the relationship. The circle was continuous, and I was constantly jumping out of the box while staying in the circle.

Not all students were as comfortable and excited about my unorthodox instructional strategies and activities as Scott and Amber. Some were so accustomed to playing the school game with worksheets, looking up vocabulary, copying notes, and being very cautious learners. My wide-open discussions, movement, and obsession to engage students took weeks for students to accept and even longer for students to put into practice the thinking required for active participation in the class. Not all students responded as well as some, but even the less enthusiastic eventually participated and went along with the rest of the class. It was also a process to get the students accustomed to my classroom assessments. No longer did they find simple multiple-choice questions, word banks, matching, and other simple recall assessment devices on tests. I made every effort and spent hours to match the assessments to the instruction the students were encountering in the lessons. Of course, the tests had an essay at the end of each exam, and I would not take an exam from a student until the essay was completed. Just as in my internship, students were taught how to write a thesis paper and required to complete one each grading period. As in the internship, the paper project was successful, and the students for the most part loved to write them.

Throughout our studies, I made sure students knew I was working hard for them. I always got papers graded quickly, and thesis papers were graded and returned in a matter of days. I have known some teachers who hold essays for weeks and weeks and return them after the grading period. The hard work of the students had to be matched by me - the "we" relationship. I remember one Friday, the deadline to submit thesis papers arrived, and students were asking if I would have the papers graded and back to them on Monday. I asked them if they thought I was Superman and had nothing else to do over the weekend. I calculated the number of hours it would take to get them all graded and announced that even I could not get all the grading done in one weekend. On Monday, the students in each class asked if I had gotten the papers graded. I was not going to miss my chance. I again told them how much time would be required and that extraordinary efforts would have been required. I played it for every ounce I could get out of it, reached in the drawer, and took out the student papers. For weeks, the students called me Super Teacher. It was an exhausting feat, and rarely did I exhibit the energy or time to grade that many essays in a weekend. I did accomplish my goal of demonstrating my commitment to the students. Whenever I expected something extra from them, I always referred back to the time I graded all those papers in a weekend. Teaching involves a great deal of psychology or manipulation - whatever you want to call it.

The Inside Struggle

The term *infanticide* refers to mature animals of the same species killing the young animals. *Filial infanticide* refers to cases in which animals kill their own young. All forms of infanticide are usually associated in some way to competition among the mature or parent animal. For example, a male of a species may kill the offspring of a female in order for the female to be available to the male. Some teachers do not appreciate other teachers who put in extra effort or get too much attention for improving teaching and learning. The unfortunate practice is especially harmful to beginning teachers who are looked at negatively if the administration, parents, or students begin to expect the same from all teachers. I acknowledge that I was different from any other teacher at my school, and because of being different, I received a great deal of attention and created a considerable amount of talk within the school, even my school with over one hundred faculty members. One thing about students is that they love to talk about teachers - to each other, to parents, and to other teachers. The absolute worst thing a student can say to a teacher is how to teach the class, and especially to teach it like some other teacher.

As I have mentioned, there was always something on a large scale going on in all my classes, and the news was always spreading by both the students and by me. One thing about people who operate outside the norm is that they do not mind telling others what is going on and care very little if it disrupts others. My instruction was getting attention, and some of my colleagues were less than enthusiastically supportive, even though my tactics were producing very good results. When informal meetings happened on my hall, in faculty meetings, and in the cafeteria, the subject of activities going on in my class caused considerable discussion. I often heard some of the veteran teachers say that my enthusiasm would wane and eventually go away when I had been there as long as they had. Another example involved the student surveys of political events and an African-American colleague expressing concern and denouncing the analysis of the survey results based on race. He concluded that continuing the practice would cause major race issues at the school.

These types of comments only motivated me more. Understand, part of my passion was not only to invest in my students, but also to bring about what I considered needed change in my profession. The passion for change in the profession would be a determining factor in my decision in later seeking a career adjustment to administration. In any event, the television exposure, students talking to others about what we did in class, parents hearing unusual positive comments about a class, and the school administration taking notice were all making many traditionalists uneasy, and I was enjoying every minute of it.

I am not implying that all my colleagues disliked me, but I did feel I was threatening the status quo. Regardless of a few deep-cutting remarks, I think most teachers were confused, amused, or curious about my style. To be honest, most teachers and administrators were very encouraging. As a result, the faculty in 1994 chose me to represent the school as a candidate for the *Alabama Teacher of the Year* and *Jacksonville State Teacher Hall of Fame* awards. I like to think I was nominated for all the right reasons and not just because I was one of a few who would actually complete the long application procedures. Regardless of the motive, I would represent my school in the secondary division and then be selected as the system nominee for the Jacksonville State recognition. In addition, the school allowed the senior class to select the senior favorite teacher each year, and it was especially moving to receive the award for three straight years. The plaques now adorn the wall in my office.

For a couple of years, I developed and taught a law class called *Law and Society*. The class involved street law concepts, and the students and I learned a great deal from the experience. We did legal briefs, conducted numerous mock trials, and had judges, lawyers, businesspersons, and law students in the classes constantly. Managing guest speakers for the class before the days of cell phones and email was a monumental task, and I spent a great deal of time on the phone in the teacher's lounge and in the office diligently trying to contact busy judges and lawyers who are difficult to get on the phone. In 1993, the Tuscaloosa Bar Association awarded me the *Liberty Bell Award* for my efforts at teaching the Constitution and rule of law. That plaque is also on display in my office.

Just Give Them the Facts

During the early and mid-1990s, I was personally very fortunate that there were relatively few guidelines laid out for teachers, and as a result there were few restrictions on my philosophy and practice in teaching. My passion for teaching and learning drove me to perform as best I could with my talent. The work ethic I possessed, along with various experiences I had before going into the classroom, created in me a sense of responsibility to set a very high standard both for me and my students. The preparation and training in methodology by several professors in undergraduate school revealed to me that learning was an active endeavor, and that passive teaching and learning would fail to achieve the results I expected for my students and for myself. I have serious reservations that given the changes in the education environment since 2001, I would have the required time or patience to teach as successfully as I did prior to *No Child Left Behind.*

The educational culture during the 90s included teachers who taught with energy and passion, along with teachers who lacked motivation and skill. A general attitude was to teach students who wanted to learn and tolerate those that were not motivated. As a result, the dropout rate in high schools was very high, and many who did graduate left school with few academic skills. Some students completed school because of social promotion. The value of education in obtaining a decent job had not been very important to many of the parents of students, but the workplace was changing and eventually dramatically reshaping the skills and training necessary to find a good job. The United States would become part of a world economy with manufacturing jobs exported to less developed nations and technology replacing many jobs that once required human labor. The job I had at the muffler plant no longer existed, and the plant where I had once worked, along with thousands more like it, were closing the doors, and thousands of employees were losing their jobs.

Very suddenly, the nation and our education system discovered the student products we were producing were not prepared for productive employment in the new economy. Just as Sputnik had shocked the nation in 1957, the economic changes would awaken educators and policy makers. Once again, the cry went out that our students were ill-prepared to compete with students from other nations, especially in math and science. If the crisis was not addressed, we risked becoming a second rate economic power in the global economy. Policymakers, most of whom were not educators, explored and debated options, and the result was the passing of the *No Child Left Behind Act of 2001*. The law mandated that by 2014, every child in public education would reach a proficiency level that would make our workforce once again the most skilled and prepared in the world. In order for states to continue to receive federal dollars for education, each school and system had to make annual progress that would hypothetically result in all students achieving an assigned proficiency level as determined from standardized achievement tests administered by the states. The thinking of the policymakers was that the test results would hold each teacher, administrator, school, and system accountable for improving student achievement.

School systems in Alabama and other states instituted a variety of standardized tests for various grade levels and an exit exam administered first in the tenth grade. Each test administration produced data that was disaggregated based on gender, race, special education, and income. Not only did each school have to meet continually increasing benchmark scores, each subgroup was required to benchmark. The disaggregated exit, or graduation exam, required each student to pass each section on math, reading, social studies, science, and language. Graduation required a student to pass all five sections of the exam. The status of high schools reflected progress from each subgroup in each learning area combined with the pass rate on the exit exam.

Just as I was concluding my years in the classroom, the state began requiring teachers to teach each subject's course of study and to document the date of the lesson that covered the objective on each teacher's lesson plan. Teachers began a practice of documentation of learning objectives that continued and increased over the next fifteen years. I heard teachers state emphatically that they would cover each objective regardless of the outcome for students. The feverish attempt to teach and document every objective in a course of study resulted from information from system and state administrators declaring that continued employment of a teacher depended on covering the objectives. Having to cover every objective sacrificed the depth of study for each discipline by expecting students to memorize enough information and facts to hopefully be able to recall on the standardized tests. Schools and teachers gave up on depth of study and focused on breadth of study. Teachers felt there was no longer any time for projects and activities that required student thinking or creativity. Schools became factories that produced many simple products.

No Child Left Behind dramatically focused learning on memorization, recall, and test taking. The mission and the purpose of schools became to teach in order for students to pass tests and provided little if any time for students to think and solve problems. Teachers became disseminators of facts, figures, and dates. Giving the graduation exam and other benchmark tests multiple times during the year, along with the requirement for ultimate test security, produced the loss of many instructional days and learning opportunities. Remediating students who had not passed one or more sections of the graduation exam and practicing to take tests also took away instructional days. Teachers and schools became obsessed with tests and rightfully so because every child in the school had to meet proficiency, and every child had to graduate. The reputation of every school, administrator, and teacher depended on the scores from the assessments. As the curriculum continued to broaden and testing became more common, teacher frustration and resignation increased, and passion for teaching decreased. Any "outside the box" teachers became file clerks with no time to reflect, students lost opportunities to be creative, and assembly-line practices whitewashed learning. Removing opportunities for students to get actively involved in learning because of time issues restricts great teachers from using the tools that made them great teachers. Is it any wonder that we often lost the most gifted teachers in the profession? I can only imagine, but faced with the same state and NCLB requirements while I was in the classroom, I would not have been an effective teacher and in frustration would probably have left the profession.

Without a doubt, the efforts to improve schools with the NCLB legislation did a great deal of harm to education. However, I concede there were some positive outcomes from the law. Educators actually began to address the issue of discounting certain populations of students based on race and socioeconomic reasons. The tests illustrated areas where deficiencies existed, and although the tests did not necessarily reflect actual specific learning, they did identify groups who performed poorly in academic areas in general. NCLB forced schools and systems to realize and accept that learning must be for all students. Many schools did improve from analyzing assessment data and implementing plans to improve. Unfortunately, however, there were also several major cases of improprieties and cheating in some schools and systems in order to inflate test scores. The damage done to instructional practice as a result of NCLB reinforced old traditions of assembly line teaching and reduced the opportunity for innovative and creative teachers to use instructional practices that produce quality learning. No Child Left Behind emphasized errant strategies and practices for fifteen years, and although some outcomes of the legislation produced some improvement, the achievement gap between students from the United States and as many as twenty-seven other countries still exists.

SIX

Instructional leadership has always been my strength. My passion for instruction enhanced my teaching practice, as well as my association with other people who excel in teaching and learning. The most significant event that shaped my instructional mind was the Advanced Placement training I received during the summer at the beginning of my teaching career. It was in the workshops where I learned, and later put into my practice in all my classes, the concept of presenting multiple texts that required student focus and creativity in order to apply the learning and to propose solutions to situations and problems presented in high-level assessments. The workshops reinforced my concept of writing as the device for students to demonstrate proficiency in an area of study. I also realized that high-level learning, partnered with constant formal and informal assessments of equally demanding caliber, offered students the opportunity to demonstrate mastery of the subject. In the simplest terms, my vision for the ultimate goal in education is to teach students to think in order to answer questions to which they do not know the answer but have to figure out. My philosophy is to promote thinking by asking provoking questions that force students to consider all sides of an issue or problem. All these strategies started twenty-five years ago in the workshops and summarize the learning philosophy I employed in my classrooms for seven years following the training.

The same ideas about learning that I practiced years ago reflect what research and experts on learning advocate and encourage today. In effect, the AP model was a precursor to the style of teaching advocated today. What successful AP teachers have done for years is just now getting to the forefront of accepted teaching and learning. Why has it taken so long?

The most tangible excuse I have for our current lack of academic achievement is the *No Child Left Behind Act.* The requirements of the law forced teachers to abandon the idea of teaching kids how to think and apply knowledge, to simply knowing enough factual answers to do well on poorly developed assessments that measured learning at the lowest end of the Bloom's learning scale. For thirteen years, students learned to take tests that merely checked for knowledge and comprehension rather than application, analysis, synthesis, and evaluation. Now with the development and implementation of Common Core Standards or other state standards based on Common Core, we are attempting to put back on track the proper way to teach students in a way that will enable them to innovatively solve problems and make our world better. In effect, our goal should be more about teaching students how to use what they know instead of just teaching them what TO know. The Common Core way of teaching and learning is nothing new, for what was once new, became old, and is now new again. I am thankful for the opportunity I had to invest actively in the development of my philosophy of teaching and learning by becoming an AP teacher. That philosophy is the foundation of my efforts today to end the NCLB mindset and to encourage instruction and learning based on thinking and problem solving.

Can You Hear Me Now?

Throughout the course of my career, my passion and determination have been to improve not only the students for whom I am responsible but to also have a meaningful impact on the profession that others and I have invested so much time and energy to employ. As I have stated before, teaching and learning constitute a calling for me. The experience I have gained from my time in the classroom and my association with hundreds of teachers, administrators, and college personnel have shaped me in a positive way. There are too many educators who have spent as much time and energy in the profession as I have who have lost enthusiasm and sometimes become condescending and negative. Since the time I was old enough to begin thinking beyond a basic cognitive level, I have spent time reflecting on observations I have made in just about every area of my life. I have often communicated my conclusions as a student, teacher, and administrator. Often, I felt a little like the man on the old cell phone television commercial who found himself in out-of-the-way places and asking, "Can you hear me now?" Unlike the person in the commercial, more often than not, no one heard me. My passion sometimes gets the best of me, which may be a flaw that prevents me from influencing as much change as quickly as I want. People not hearing me has been and remains the biggest source of frustration in my career.

I am very proud of my career, but I am most proud of my years in the classroom because I feel I was ahead of my time in my philosophy of and practice in teaching and learning. Despite the years I have spent observing and having to react to guidelines and mandates from ineffectual educational practice dictated by poor legislation, I continue to be a representative for change in how we teach and run schools. I find it somewhat gratifying that what I learned many years ago from Pat Ferguson and Cecelia Pierce in my undergraduate methodology class that was reinforced and enhanced from the AP workshops, is almost identical to the ideas about teaching and learning advocated today. The same obstacles I faced as a teacher and the misguided practices associated with NCLB are very much still in practice. Based on my many experiences and observations, and from my current position as an instructional leader, I recognize several common practices that must and will change if educators properly prepare students for challenges each will face in his or her life.

My earlier conclusion that parents today do all or most of the thinking for the children by planning and organizing activities coupled with teaching that fails to provoke curiosity and demand high-level thinking creates a student product poorly prepared for a successful career. My stepson is a systems engineer with Northrop Grumman, a major high-technology industry with facilities in our area and around the world. The title of his position is *Solutions*

Architect. In the position, he not only has to develop innovative solutions to problems that exist in the industry, he also faces the task of thinking of problems that may develop and plan for solutions in the event a problem does arise. His education and training have provided him with necessary tools to use in implementing strategies, but there is no way his education and training could cover every problem he will encounter in his job. He was fortunate to have exceptional ability, which provided him the opportunity to take advanced classes where he participated in projects and activities that required him and his team to work toward a solution. His mom and I have had serious conversations with him on how his education prepared him for the role he now plays. Without hesitation, his response consistently includes the experience from his classes that stimulated his interest and provoked an innate passion for facing a challenging issue that forced him to find an answer to a problem for which there was no answer in the book or on the internet.

What has made our country strong has always been innovation and creativity. Unfortunately, common teaching practices often stifle creativity. Just like my stepson, my daughter's gifted and advanced classes encouraged thought and problem solving and prepared her for her professional career. We spend too much classroom time on management that is often the result of dictates from the federal government to the local administration. We have not abandoned the concept of mass education in an assembly line process. There should be little difference in teaching and learning in gifted and regular classes because every child possesses giftedness in some area. Scott was not in gifted classes, and most teachers expected nothing but negative issues from him. However, by opening the door to his imagination and allowing him to think and explore, his many talents were exposed and nurtured. In order to prepare students for the twenty-first century, education must promote and provide continual practice in thinking outside the box and solving problems.

Effective teaching and learning requires a collaborative effort between the teacher and the students, as well as among the students. Teachers must prepare motivating, provoking, and engaging lessons that demonstrate the "I, you, and we" relationship. Teachers must continually demonstrate a commitment to teaching and learning. Some of the best classroom experiences I had were when I was probably too sick to be at school. The fact I was there sick indicated to the students the importance I placed on learning, and they always responded positively. I have to deal with some teachers who place little value on the responsibility of teaching students. A number of the teachers are out of the class too often on sick, personal, or professional leave provided to them from various sources, including the state. School system administrators often schedule that holiest of sacred solutions to instructional problems of professional development during instructional times. In my current system, I have concluded that time spent on actual instruction ranges only from 40% at the best and 25% at the worst. Teacher absenteeism is only a small part of the problem, but it is often a major contributing factor. The most often heard complaint from teachers regarding innovative instruction is that there is no time for it. The continued expansion of curriculum, along with duties and responsibilities associated with a massive bureaucracy, too many in-school non-curricular activities and fieldtrips, and teacher absenteeism drastically reduce opportunities for effective methodologies and student-centered teaching. If I owned a business and sold a product but spent only 25% of my time trying to sell it, I would soon be out of business.

Another issue and a leftover from NCLB is the amount of testing that still takes place in schools. I recently heard a class presentation from a group of teachers and administrators in a graduate class discuss system-wide assessments in their school. One of the discoveries of the group was that a particular testing program they had used for years did not correlate to the end-of-the-year assessment required by the state. I stopped the group as they passed up any judgment on the discovery and asked them the obvious question: "Why do you do use the test if it does not correlate to the required state test?" The answer indicated a common problem in education of always adding ingredients to the pot and never removing anything. The answer was that the system and the teachers had been using the tests long before the required final assessment, the teachers were comfortable administering the test and studying the results, and all parties just accepted the test as part of the regular school curriculum. It is time to dispense of the things in education that do not work. Every time a new program or initiative starts, it should replace some existing program.

Formal testing in my system, and common in most systems since required by the state, is to administer end-of-the-year assessments. Assessment may not be a perfect solution for accountability, but it is the best alternative available. One test at the end of the year to me is acceptable in order to determine if learning has occurred and to make the teacher, school, and system accountable. The College Board Exam in my AP classes was my accountability measure. However, systems are now also getting heavily involved and spending millions of dollars with companies that specialize in what they refer to as formative assessments that are administered from one to five times during the school year. In actuality, formative assessments should be continual and immediate. The so-called formative assessments given periodically in school systems are actually interim assessments and provide no timely feedback to teachers. Each test administration may take a day or up to a week. The purpose of the data from the tests is to ascertain the competency of the students in mastering the standards and is diagnostic and rarely prescriptive. Personnel spend days and weeks breaking the data down to diagnose how well the students did at a particular grade level and subject. The tests are expensive and discouraging since the amount of time meant for instruction spent on testing students to measure growth dramatically reduces the amount of time for learning. The process is a vicious cycle and compounded when systems employ more and more testing. Many tests assess students on how well they will perform on other tests. As an old adage goes, weighing the hog more does not make it gain weight.

Another common educational practice often mentioned in improvement plans and initiatives is professional development training for teachers. Professional growth is vitally important in any profession, and state certification regulations require teachers to accumulate continuous education units (CEUs) in order to maintain certification. However, the educational bureaucracy, product and program training, and testing analysis meetings require large amounts of time for teachers to be out of class and in meetings. A common reaction when a test identifies a deficiency in student learning is for the system to provide professional development and training for teachers. A school system flooded with professional development removes teachers from the classroom, reduces instructional time, increases the pace when the teacher returns and attempts to make up for lost time, and reduces the depth of instruction and learning. Losing instructional time, along with an obsession to cover the entire course of study, also eliminates opportunities for active learning activities that require more time for planning and implementation.

Requiring all training after school, on weekends, and in the summer reduces the loss of instructional time. Unfortunately, teachers participating in training at non-instructional times require teacher compensation for the time in training. Still, paying for a substitute and the spillover cost of lost instructional time far outweigh the cost of stipends for professional development training sessions.

Testing, along with data analysis and professional development, is a lingering effect of NCLB in that the practices are an attempt to make teaching a science. In looking at teaching as a science, the art often goes overlooked and is lost in an effort to improve student achievement. In addition, fulfilling duties associated with a scientific approach to teaching and learning forces teachers who possess the art of teaching to abandon the art to focus on stacks of regulations and data. Less time for instruction eliminates time for depth in learning and maintains the NCLB practices and outcomes. Student-centered and active learning requires more time and produces students who can think and problem solve. Yet, we continue to reduce time for instruction, and the results produce unmotivated students and teachers, unskilled thinkers, and poor-performing students. Until teachers are given the time to provide innovative teaching strategies that engage students and teach them to think, efforts to improve learning and better prepare students for college and a career will fail. We must make wise investments.

The Key Ingredient

Every chef knows that the key to any great recipe is to use the best ingredients. Preparation and presentation of a dish are important, but failing to use good ingredients will produce marginal results. Sometimes when I want to cook spaghetti, I stand at the meat counter and look at the varieties of ground beef products from ground beef to ground round. The ground round or sirloin look so alluring without fat and with the beautiful red color we associate with freshness and quality. However, I have discovered from experience that the more lean products lack the flavor provided by the fat found in the ground beef or chuck. The right ingredients produce the best results. In order for instruction and learning in schools to produce the best results, we must start with good ingredients. Since all students can learn at some level given the opportunity and given the fact that we have no choice on the ability or quality of students who walk through the schoolhouse door, the only variable we can control is the teacher.

In my current position, I have seen as many as 400 applicants for open teaching positions. In my state, there are as many as 10,000 certified teachers looking for jobs at any given time. Record numbers of students are graduating from college with teaching degrees. A disappointing notion in colleges among students is that if a student fails in engineering, medicine, business, or any other degree field, there is always teaching as a last resort. The bottom line is that the profession is often not attracting the best or most talented people to become educators. Some of the education graduates are students who were unable to graduate in other fields of study. A look at the countries where students outperform ours indicates that citizens hold the teaching profession in very high regard, and the requirements to become a teacher are as strenuous as in any other field of study. Finland, for example, has rigorous qualifications and achievement standards for teacher candidates and requires five years of study and preparation. From the thousands of applicants for preparation as teachers in Finland, only 15% begin the rigorous preparation and training. The study requires tremendous dedication and ability from the candidates to achieve a certificate. The study involves research and application of innovative methodologies and practices designed to encourage innovative and creative instruction. In most universities and colleges in the United States, there are few requirements to enter a teacher preparation program other than basic competency and minimal grade point averages. Too many of the teachers we are putting in classrooms are teachers for the wrong reasons and are ill-prepared; therefore, we are failing to use the highest quality ingredients that are needed for successful schools.

Recently, I visited the Ron Clark Academy in Atlanta and saw teaching and learning as I have never before experienced. One of the many things I observed was that no student was using any form of technology. The teaching and learning resembled a model of reflective and mutual discourse very similar to a style of a prominent teacher named Socrates. The focus in the classroom was dialogue with the teacher and among the students. Students were arguing assertions and defending their conclusions in every subject and class. From my perspective, my most apparent defining conclusion was that the major factor for the success of the majority disadvantaged, inner-city students was the teachers. The emphasis at the academy is on student engagement, and the teachers were experts. The success of the academy is the result of extremely highly qualified teachers who had a gift for teaching, were unencumbered by bureaucracy, engaged students at the highest level of thinking, and encouraged finding solutions to real-world problems.

The lack of rigor in teacher education programs and employment recruitment creates a dilemma similar to the dog chasing his tail analogy. The low expectations we have for teacher candidates produce teachers with low expectations for students. Many of these students will then become teacher candidates, and the cycle is established. There are of course exceptions to the pattern, but reiterating a previous point, the frustration of high quality teachers associated with bureaucratic mandates and unproductive practices discourages and prevents our best teachers from using their gifts. Again, I was fortunate in my practice to avoid jumping through hoops and participating in extraneous activities. Fewer non-instructional responsibilities allowed me to use my talent, passion, and energy to teach. We must select great teachers, train them, protect instructional time, and provide teachers with the opportunity to teach.

The practices and bad habits accumulated from NCLB for the last fifteen years, and the transition to an educational culture that supports the art of teaching will not happen quickly. The generation of teachers preparing now for employment provides hope for the future. My recruiting efforts at universities and colleges are giving me hope that some of our postsecondary schools are doing a much better job at preparing students to be teachers. School and system administrators must, however, be able to recognize and attract the best teachers. The efforts of higher education developing rigorous and valid teacher preparation programs combined with public educators recruiting, hiring, and supporting the best candidates will slowly turn the tide on a major obstacle to education reform.

The Rx Mentality

I am a news fanatic. Except for a few select television shows, the cable and network news programs dominate my time in front of the television. I have observed over the last several years that it seems a majority of the sponsors for news shows are drug companies promoting particular drugs for every ailment known to man. I assume the same advertisements are common on all television shows. I have also become acquainted with many medical issues I did not know existed. With a vast array of prescription medications, we are increasingly expectant that proper medication reduces the symptoms of almost any medical issue we may encounter. The pill solution is also evident by the number of drug stores that are located on seemingly every corner of every populated community. Although I am completely in favor of advancements in medications for relieving human suffering, I think we are equating treating symptoms of disease over prevention. Perhaps we should do a better job of listening to the medical professionals and take personal responsibility in addressing our habits and lifestyles in preventing medical issues. Instead, many of us eat poorly, exercise very little, abuse our bodies, and then expect the doctor to give us a medication to cure us. In so many ways, we have come to expect all problems to have quick fixes and easy solutions. Is it better to build a building or a bridge correctly than to spend resources in the future repairing problems with the construction? Instead of expending resources on methods of repair, we must balance resources to deal with problems that currently exist, along with investing in ways to prevent those problems in the future.

Every problem diagnosed in education results in the bombardment of educators from multiple angles with a variety of repair resources or remedies. Every marketing maneuver targets teachers and administrators. The natural reaction is the same that exists in the prescription drug mentality. In effect, here is our problem, and we will use this particular product or program to fix the disease. The attempts to repair the problems are noble, but I fear we too often sacrifice prevention measures because teachers are required to spend increasingly amounts of time repairing oversights and damage. As a result, teachers have less time to actually teach and ensure student competency, invest in ways to improve instruction and learning, and reduce the need for repairs in the future.

The result of our repair way of thinking in education is that most resources of time and money utilize external investments in programs and plans. I firmly believe that educators realize that we could do a better job at providing instruction that reduces panic and results in less of an emphasis on repair programs, yet the pressure to correct mistakes focuses most efforts toward treating the symptoms. Perhaps a better approach would be to focus on internal investments. Internal investments include students, teachers, and administrators. My rescue from a cycle that produced a lack of motivation and achievement was not the result of a new instructional methodology, technology, or emphasis on math and science. What saved me was the investment from people who encouraged and provided a model for me to recognize and determine that dedication and perseverance produces success. Many of the factors outside of school that influenced me are not as prevalent today. Therefore, education must accept the responsibility of investing in students who do not have anything but teachers who can play a positive role in promoting individual achievement and ultimate success. Individual students and his or her future should be the primary focus of all education policy and practice. Policy makers and school systems must provide time and opportunity for teachers to teach with passion, rigor, and relevance. Every student must recognize a genuine determination by each teacher, coach, counselor, and administrator to provide training and guidance that produce dividends for each student. Education must be personal and not clinical. Each student must feel that every lesson and concept is an investment in his or her future. Education reform will not happen from external investments but from internalizing every effort toward the individual student.

Dividends

In writing this book, I have recalled and reflected on the many people and events that have shaped my life and provided me with what I consider the basis for my career and purpose in life. Although I have mentioned instances and people that have been important to me, the accounts are just a representation of the enumerable factors that most influenced and motivated me in my journey. Without a doubt the investment, encouragement, and example made by so many has delivered me to a point in my life where I am at least satisfied with what I have accomplished. There is so much more I wish I had done, but any setbacks or failures I have experienced were mostly my fault and pale in comparison to the joy and fulfillment I have enjoyed. I was not a perfect teacher, but I do feel I came close to doing my best, and my passion and dedication to teaching and learning are unquestionable. As I have endeavored to convey my journey by looking back at my life, I can see how everything in my life fits together, and all I have observed and experienced have made me who I am and what I do.

I am thankful for my humble beginnings. Although the experience was painful at the time, my personal motivation to escape poverty created a desire in me to find an avenue of escape. My mother's hard work to provide for two young boys, and the decision to provide my brother and me an association with people interested in investing in us provided us the best opportunity to succeed. Her investment was primarily in her sons. I will forever be grateful for her love and direction. Until just before she passed away, her direction and guidance for her children with her unselfish and giving personality helped to assure our well-being. She was very proud of me but no more than I was proud of her giving to me all she had to give. The greatest gift she gave me was the ability to see the good in others and how investing in my children, as well as my students and myself, produced dividends. She too was not without faults, but her sacrifices and encouragement overshadowed all imperfections.

My father had a similar effect on my life. Although estranged from me for many years, he changed his life and became a good father and grandfather. He taught me about the honor of hard work and the importance of modeling a strong work ethic in order to motivate and lead others to do the same. Growing up in a coal mine community of West Virginia and being the descendent of several generations of miners, serving his country in Korea, battling and defeating an alcohol addiction, and finally being a good father made me realize that no matter the circumstances, there is good in everyone. As an educator, part of my mission is to help students find the good inside themselves and to recognize, develop, and utilize their gifts.

Many people have invested in me with encouragement and expressions of confidence in my abilities. My church was probably the most dramatic outside influence, especially the several people within the church I have identified in my acknowledgement. These people lifted me up and revealed a path that was achievable for me. Most importantly, they accepted, coached, and set an example of how to express real faith with actions and not just words. Additionally, my father-in-law, who demonstrated perseverance, consistency, organization, and planning, led me through his example. In the classroom, I attempted to follow what I had learned from the people who had actively invested in me and to demonstrate my commitment and dedication to students with my actions.

My employment experiences taught me how to work with a variety of individuals in various environments. My first supervisor at the A&P illustrated to me that young people often make mistakes, and that as adults and educators, we must recognize poor decisions and have the patience to forgive and help students learn and grow from mistakes. My association with the workers on the farm vividly revealed to me that all people are gifted. I am convinced that each one of the workers had multiple talents in areas beyond and different from mine. For many reasons, education had failed these people. Had the farm workers experienced learning based on his interests and applied learning directly to those interests while in school, the future would have been much brighter for each of them. What a difference we could make in human development and productivity if we would match students to their area of interest and prepare them in a specific use of learning that enhances their abilities. Instead, we often revert to the assembly line model and seek to mass-produce a standardized student product. Unfortunately, we talk about relevance in education, but we rarely invest in real application for learning that produces practical and productive dividends.

Dividends result from good investments. The success I have had in my career, my philosophy about life and learning, and any contribution I have made to my profession are the result of investments made in me by so many people. I hope that people I have been fortunate enough to teach and work with in my career and have influenced in a positive way illustrate my dividends. I consider my personal dividends in the satisfaction that I made choices that reflected the guiding investments made by family, church members, colleagues, coaches, and teachers. My prayer is that others have seen me as I see the people who invested in me, and that those investments will create even greater dividends for them and for me.